Discover a
Lovelier You

DP The Danbury Press

WOMAN ALIVE

Discover a Lovelier You

by Ann Craig

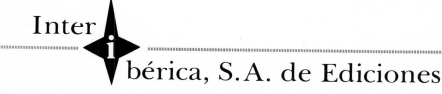

Inter **i** bérica, S.A. de Ediciones

Series Coordinator: John Mason
Design Director: Guenther Radtke
Picture Editor: Peter Cook
Copy Editor: Mitzi Bales
Research: Marion Pullen
         Ann Reading
         Lynette Trotter
Consultants: Beppie Harrison
            Elizabeth Kendall
            Jo Sandilands

Contents

Beauty—today, that one little word has as many facets as a diamond. It means fashion magazines, models, and movie stars. It means a thousand and one products and services, from cosmetics and the latest fashions, to hair stylists and figure experts. It even means controversy, at least to a few members of Women's Lib, who say that womanly beauty is overstressed. But the desire to be attractive is as natural and timeless as human nature itself. The only vital thing is that caring for your looks should give you pleasure. This book, then, takes a fresh and happy approach to skin and hair care, make-up and clothes, diet and exercise. And, as a bonus, there's a chapter on the intriguing relationship between looks and self-image, and an in-depth report on cosmetic surgery.

What is Beauty?

Different times, different countries, different lives—each has, or had, its own particular character, and each has contributed to the ever-changing concept of beauty.

Right: in Ancient Egypt, more than 1,300 years before the birth of Christ, the stylized features of Queen Nefertiti set the trend.

Left: for Renaissance Italians, to be blonde was to be beautiful, and many dark Italian women dyed their hair to achieve this ideal.

Below: today, we see beauty as an individual quality, transcending national frontiers.

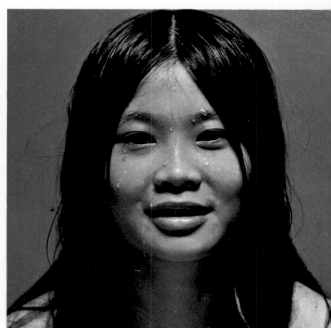

Below: some of the African peoples find beauty in adornment, especially jewelry. This Masai woman, for example, wears innumerable necklaces, bangles, and ear rings.

Right: our more sophisticated society has evolved the concept of "public" beauty, a glamour associated above all with a star. For many, this image spells Sophia Loren.

Below right: for most of us, the ideal now is natural beauty, springing from a glow of health, vitality, and self-contentment.

The Changing Shape of Beauty

As fashion changes, our ideas follow after, and our concept of what is beautiful alters in their wake. At different times, fashion has emphasized different ideal body shapes.

Below: the Venus de Milo, in its closeness to nature, represents the Greek classical ideal.

Right: in Spain, in the 1600's, dresses were padded to give the impression of wide hips.

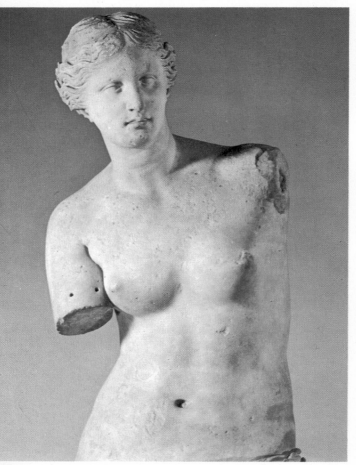

Right: the paintings of the French artist Ingres show that by the 1800's the emphasis had moved upward, and high waistlines were concentrating attention on the bust.

Above: later in the 1800's, the point of interest moved backward, as skirts were gathered back over hoops called bustles to exaggerate the size of the bottom.

Right: the "modern woman" of the 1920's found corsets outdated, and rejected the curvy female line of the 1800's. The fashion ideal was to be slender, and the boyish look—with a flat chest—reigned supreme.

Far right: in the 1960's, men became happily addicted to fashion, as the popularity of the mini-skirt showed more and more leg.

Crowning Glory

Below: the myriad ways in which women have worn their hair have been an endless source of fascination to the men around them. To the Renaissance artist Botticelli, the most ravishing style of all was a free-flowing mass of tresses—Nature personified.

Right: another Renaissance artist, Leonardo da Vinci, here captures the simple elegance of a more severe and restrained hair style.

Right: 18th-century ladies had elaborate coiffures of real and artificial hair together, decorated with ribbons, plumes, and flowers.

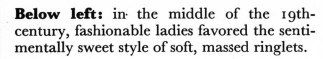

Below left: in the middle of the 19th-century, fashionable ladies favored the sentimentally sweet style of soft, massed ringlets.

Left: during the 1920's, women exploited their greater social freedom by cutting their hair short—the famous boyish bob, which both scandalized and intrigued the men.

Below: although fashion directives change from year to year, vast numbers of young women now wear their hair in the most natural style of all, loose and straight. It's back to Botticelli's Renaissance ideal, in fact!

The Tools of Beauty

Nature may lay the foundations of beauty, but throughout the centuries, women, no matter how beautiful, have always done their best to give nature a kind helping hand.

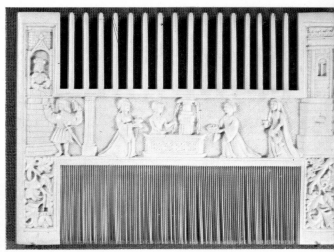

Left: a woman of 2,000 years ago having her hair done, in a painting from Pompeii.

Above: this medieval comb, carved from ivory, is a thing of beauty in itself.

Below and right: coloring the lips is probably one of the oldest of beauty tricks.

Left: the world of the Orient has had a special fascination for many Westerners, and the demure beauty of the Japanese women must surely have been part of the appeal.

Below left: the casual, outdoorsy beauty of a Celtic redhead, spangled with freckles.

Below: the woman of the 20th century is free, as few of her ancestors were, to work out her own approach to beauty.

Self-Image, The Key to Your Looks

1

Have you ever longed to be absolutely, ravishingly beautiful? What woman hasn't! The desire to be beautiful—or at least without noticeable imperfections—seems to be as universal among women as the desire to succeed is among men. But *why* do we want to be beautiful?

For most of us, the wish is so deeply ingrained that we rarely stop to think about it. But when we do, three rather potent reasons spring to mind: first, of course, to be desirable, to please and appeal to the opposite sex—in a word, to win and keep the men we love. Second (and let's be honest), to compete successfully with other women, whether they be the ones we actually know, or simply the ones we see on TV, in the movies, and on the pages of every magazine. Last, but certainly not least, to please ourselves, to feel that special inner glow of knowing we look great.

But *should* we want to be beautiful? We all know what the most militant members of Women's Lib feel on this score. Germaine Greer, for example, laid it on the line in a lively *Playboy* interview. "Why," she demanded, "should women's bodies be this sort of physical fetish? Why can't their bodies just be an extension of their personalities, the way a man supposes his body is?" In a pamphlet called *Our Bodies, Our Selves,* members of the Boston Women's Health Course Collective put it this way: "Why this frantic search for beauty? The slightest so-called imperfection is a source of private anxiety and fear. We view our bodies and those of other women according to how closely they measure up to the sexist standards of society. Why is this crippling us? Because we are forced to be preoccupied by how we appear to others

Your kind of beauty is a highly individual asset, made up of the way you move, the way you are seen to respond, and the way you feel—as well as the way you look. Beauty can never be defined by a single, rigid, standard, for there will always be as many ways of being beautiful as there are women in the world.

At the beginning, all of us experiment uncertainly with the paraphernalia of feminine adornment—and who can't remember the delight and excitement of staring into a mirror at a face that is clearly your own, but subtly changed by the unfamiliar magic of the lipstick.

rather than be concerned by how we feel from within."

Is there anything in what the militants say? *No,* if what they really mean is that we should neglect our looks entirely, just let ourselves go, and devote our energies to self-expression. *Yes,* insofar as they have laid bare our hangups about beauty, and challenged the idea that any woman should feel guilty and anxious about the way she's put together. *Yes,* insofar as they have shown just how joyless and competitive excessive concern with beauty can be. *Yes,* insofar as they have pointed out how little we accept ourselves as we are, how frequently we actively dislike our bodies or parts of our bodies.

The militants will never convince women to abandon their interest in beauty. Nor should they. Any woman with the capacity

for enjoying life wants to please, wants to excite interest, wants to feel the sheer exhilaration of knowing that—as the Bible puts it so beautifully—"she is good to look upon." The desire to be physically attractive is as natural and instinctive, in men as well as women, as the desire to love and be loved.

So, in urging us to turn our backs on beauty altogether, the militant liberationists —like many revolutionaries—probably go too far. But they have helped to put things back in perspective, and—perhaps only by default—have pointed the way to a new and far more positive approach to beauty. That approach is based simply and squarely on the premise that, before we do anything else, we must like and accept ourselves. And that means all over, from head to toe.

Oddly enough, a great many of us find this

A fashion model is a practiced professional at the game of beauty. The pots and powders are her working tools, and she learns to use them to enhance her own face and figure until she stands ready for the photographer: remote, flawless, and completely sophisticated.

Even among the beauties of the stage and screen, beauty wears a thousand faces, no two alike. Left: Barbra Streisand, famous nose and all, instantly strikes her public as a proud and individual beauty. Right: Brigitte Bardot is another distinctive woman, famous as a symbol of sexy beauty.

very hard to do. Bombarded from early childhood with images of near-perfect beauty in magazines and subway ads, the movies and TV, we become convinced that there is something, or several somethings, about our looks that are imperfect, inadequate, or downright ugly.

You're too tall or too short, too fat or too thin. Your curves are not distributed the way you'd like them to be, or you have problem skin, or a prominent nose, or unmanageable hair. Moreover, as you get older—especially nowadays, with the frantic emphasis on youth—a whole new load of "imperfections" seems to assail you. It's not just the wrinkles that worry you, but the seemingly unbudgeable midriff bulge, the unwelcome appearance of varicose veins, or the allover loss of muscle tone.

The farther you are—or you get—from the "ideal" image, the more anxious and defeated you tend to feel about your looks. What you have got going for you seems as nothing compared with what you lack. In desperation, you may declare a state of war on your body, making of the problem areas a series of "battlefields," to be won with crash diets, hectic exercises, and expensive paraphernalia.

Does this sound like you? If it does, take consolation from the fact that millions of other women feel exactly the same way, and wage exactly the same battles.

What's wrong with this approach? Simply that it's basically negative. Since time began, women have experimented with exotic make-ups, elaborate hair styles, and the newest fashions, many of which were somewhat uncomfortable, if not positively ridiculous. Nonetheless, the women of past ages enjoyed playing around with the latest fads and fancies—and probably a good deal more than we do. For the plain fact is that women today have let a lot of the pleasure go out of caring for themselves, and have become a great deal more other-directed about what constitutes beauty, not only in public figures, but also in themselves.

Probably because of the pervasive influence of the mass media, our standards of beauty are far higher, more conformist, and less flexible than ever before. All this emphasis on perfection makes it very difficult for any woman to feel confident about her looks. American psychologist Albert Ellis even believes that women would have fewer psychological problems if they weren't so concerned with deficiencies of face and figure. He set up a control group of women, none of whom were in therapy, and found that all but one had feelings of inadequacy about her looks.

"My hips are too high. I don't like them. And my back's too thin . . . and—Oh—just everything, awful!"

"I'm too short of leg, too big in the arms,

The perfect figure has had a hundred different shapes through the centuries. Even now, the range of figure types considered lovely is remarkable Left: Twiggy, the ''skinny girl'' of worldwide fame. Right: Raquel Welch, a curvy Hollywood beauty.

too many chins, nose a bit crooked, big feet, big hands. I'm too fat . . . ''

"I think I'm lousy looking . . . "

Recognize the speaker in any of these self-critical remarks? Probably not, though the comments all sound familiar enough. Three average women? Only the first, an interviewee of Dr. Ellis. The second and third self-critics will surprise you: Elizabeth Taylor and Brigitte Bardot!

If even the most celebrated beauties feel dissatisfied with their looks, it's hardly astonishing that the rest of us do, too. What a depressing way of viewing ourselves it is! But what can we do about it? How can we fulfill our natural desire to be more attractive without tackling our problems like combat officers? Is there, in fact, any alternative to the drastic-remedy syndrome?

Yes, of course there is—and it's an approach that has the double advantage of being as up-to-date as Women's Lib, and as timeless as beauty itself. It rests on one simple but all-important principle: that you begin by liking yourself—all over, and without reservations. The first step is to accept yourself fully, recognizing all the attributes you were born with.

Start by taking a long, *soft* look at yourself in the mirror. Study—affectionately—all the features on your face, your basic build, your hair and skin, your hands and feet. Be generous, not hypercritical, toward the person you see in the mirror. She's a living, vulnerable human being, after all, and not a series of "problem areas." Try seeing yourself as others do—they're not half so hard to please as you are!

You don't have to be a narcissist to like and respect your own face and body. They deserve it. You are absolutely special, no one exactly like you has ever lived before, or will

ever live again. To make the most of it—and to give freely and lovingly of yourself to others—you need to feel a certain joy in your own uniqueness. Deep down, you know it makes sense; but more than that, it's vital to the well-being and good looks of the total you.

If you still have reservations about some permanent, characteristic part of yourself, it may help to remember what Francis Bacon once said, long ago in the 16th century: "There is no excellent beauty that hath not some strangeness in the proportion." (Consider Twiggy, Barbra Streisand, and Carrie Snodgrass). Remember too, if the passage of years is getting you down, the appreciative view of mature women in Stephen Vizinczey's bestselling book, *In Praise of Older Women*. Vive la difference! Not only between men and women, but between one woman and another. What a dull world this would be if we all conformed to some single, rigid standard of good looks!

Now let's suppose that you're over the first hurdle, that you've decided to like and respect your fundamental self. It then follows, as night the day, that you will cherish yourself. Every living thing benefits from concerned and gentle attention. You, no less than your husband and your children, the family pets, and the flowers in your garden, need and deserve tender loving care. Do you give it to yourself?

Think now: Do you let your hands get red and rough because you always neglect to put on rubber gloves? Do you wash your hair perfunctorily, as though it were a pair of socks? Do you hurry through your bath or shower, eat junk foods and quickie meals, go from one day to the next without drawing a single deep breath of outdoor air? Would you honestly advise someone you cared about to do the same? No one needs to be told that good health is a basic prerequisite for radiant good looks.

Now, let's take a new and enlightened approach to the whole idea of beauty. It is not—as we all know—the be-all and end-all of existence. You do not need the proportions of Raquel Welch, or the flawless complexion

Ali McGraw, with her fresh, all-American-girl, glowing complexion, represents the traditional romantic image of beauty spiced with the honest, straightforward appeal of the contemporary scene.

of Ali MacGraw, to enjoy life to the full at any age. Nor do you need the grim determination of a latter-day martyr to improve your assets.

Simply being able to make more of your looks is one of the good things of life—especially nowadays, with the wide availability of excellent beauty aids and products. But the important thing is to enjoy it, and above all, to enjoy being you. Live a little! Your own unique physical existence is a gift to be treasured. You can like yourself just as you are, or experiment with a few things that will enhance your looks and deepen your pleasure in being you. Self-enhancement is simply one of life's "optional extras"—and a delightful one at that. Basically, it should be a kind of game, in which you explore new ways of caring for yourself, expressing your individuality, and giving special pleasure to those you love.

When all is said and done, what most of us want from a book about beauty is how to bring out the best in ourselves—without spending eight hours a day at it. We none of us want to be bullied into some insanely time-consuming program of self-improvement. Nor, by the same token, do we want to be brainwashed out of caring about the way we look.

Happily, there is an excellent recipe for making the most of ourselves that lies exactly half-way between the two extremes. It is composed of one part self-acceptance, one part self-care, and one part self-enjoyment. The words "cherishing yourself" sum it all up. And this book is designed to help you do just that: to tell you just about everything you ever wanted to know about face and figure, hair and skin, make-up and fashion. It's comprehensive, and it's also up-to-date. Enjoy it!

Your Face: The Two-Way Mirror

To everyone else, your face is a living thing, changing constantly as you respond to the flow of life around you. To you, your face is most often the posed, still mask staring out of the mirror.

In many ways, your face is the most precious part of your whole body. You not only look out and speak from it, you instinctively express your innermost thoughts and strongest feelings with it. It's the first thing others notice about you, and probably the chief focus of your own self-scrutiny. Yet how well do you really know it?

Oddly enough, other people probably know your face a good deal better than you do. Why? Because they see it in motion—talking, laughing, working, loving—spontaneously reacting to all the joys and sorrows of daily life. But you know a different face—the one you see in the mirror—and, if you're like most of us, the expression reflected there is anything but spontaneous. Automatically, we all tend to adopt a pose when we look in a mirror, temporarily "arranging" our features while we put on make-up or try on a dress. But the moment we turn away from the mirror, our faces come back to life, instantaneously telegraphing our most fleeting moods and basic attitudes.

It's a good idea to keep this in mind, for the features we are born with are only half the story. They are constantly "under construction" from within, being shaped and molded by the expressions that play over them. Of course, it's impossible to look happy when you don't feel that way; but if you often find yourself frowning or scowling out of sheer habit, give a thought to the sensitive material you're working on.

What about that sensitive material? Your skin, and the delicate fabric of muscles beneath it, are something you can learn a lot about. It's vital that you should, for only by really knowing and caring for them can you

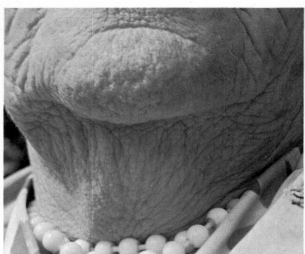

As you grow older, your skin gradually changes. A baby's skin is smooth and soft, with a thick layer of fat underneath. In old age, the skin is deeply wrinkled, mainly because of a loss of fat and of the skin's elastic fibers. These changes are sadly inevitable, but by taking good care of your skin while you're in the prime of life, you can do a lot to slow down the development of wrinkles.

make the most of your face, this fragile and all-important "mirror of your soul."

To begin at the beginning, what kind of complexion do you have: oily, dry, or average? It's surprising how many women are not really sure, but there's a very simple way of finding out. Before going to bed, wash your face thoroughly with soap and water, blot it dry, and leave it bare. In the morning, examine it closely in the mirror. Is there a glossy sheen on the surface? If there is, you probably have oily skin. To make absolutely sure, wipe one half of your face with a tissue, and then compare the two sides of your face. If there is now a big difference in the degree of gloss on the two sides, your skin is definitely oily. If the difference is only slight, you have average skin. If there is no difference at all, and, in addition, your face feels slightly tight and drawn, you have dry skin.

At this point you're probably wondering, "What about this so-called combination skin we're always reading about?" In fact, according to dermatologists, there's no such

thing. The oil-producing glands are more thickly clustered down the center panel of the face, from the forehead to the chin. So, if your skin is basically oily, it will tend to be oilier toward the center, and if it's essentially dry, it will tend to be drier away from the center. This simplifies things a lot, because it means that you have just one complexion to care for—and caring for your face is what this chapter is all about.

To start, let's talk about face care for the woman with oily skin. The most important thing she must do is keep it clean. Her skin is producing a superabundance of natural oils, and unless the pores are kept clean and clear, they will soon clog up, resulting in the blemishes we call "troubled skin."

Fortunately, oily complexions tolerate soap very well. So, if you have this type of skin, you needn't feel any qualms about washing your face thoroughly with soap and water twice a day. Before you wash your face at night, first remove your make-up with a cleansing lotion, or preferably, a cleansing milk. All such lotions contain agents especi-

Getting your face clean is important, whatever your skin type might be. Rinsing with warm, then cool, water is part of any skin cleansing routine.

ally designed to blend with the components of make-up, thus facilitating its removal.

When the last traces of make-up are gone, rinse off the lotion with cool water. Then make a rich lather of mild soap—and it should be mild however oily your complexion —and gently work it into your skin with your fingertips. Pay special attention to the center panel of your face—forehead, nose, and chin—but be sure to use, on all portions of your face, a circular and upward motion as you wash. Rinse well, first with warm, and then with cool, water, and then blot, rather than rub, dry with a towel. When dry, apply a mild freshening lotion, such as witch-hazel, to tone the skin and close the pores. Beware of harsh astringents. Though they do dry out the skin temporarily, they can also encourage it to produce even more oil than usual in sheer self-defense.

Finally, just before going to bed, apply a moisturizer. Even if you have oily skin? Yes. Oil and moisture are not the same thing, and, unless your skin is extremely oily, it is wise to replenish the natural moisture it has lost during the day.

Morning face care for the woman with oily skin should be a quick repetition of what she does at night: another washing, another dollop of skin toner, and another application of moisturizer as a make-up base.

The woman with average skin can follow the same daily face care program as the woman with oily skin— with one important exception. Her skin doesn't tolerate soap as well, so she should confine herself to a single washing with mild soap and water at bed-time. This should be done after she has removed her make-up with cleansing lotion,

either milk or cream, and before she applies the all-important moisturizer that will keep her skin looking fresh and healthy.

Now, what about face care for the dry complexion? If your skin is dry, your watch-word must be to avoid soap as much as you can. If you find you must use soap occasionally to remove deep-down dirt and grime, make sure it's the mildest of the mild—a superfatted, or baby soap. You should also be very sparing in your use of skin toners. Don't make them a regular feature of your face care. It's all right, though, to use them once in a while to give your skin that tingly feeling of allover freshness.

On a regular basis, the woman with dry skin should rely mainly on cleansing creams to remove her make-up. Afterward, the cream should be rinsed off with warm, then cool, water (preferably softened) and then gently blotted dry. We've all heard it said that women with dry skin shouldn't use water on their faces, but it's often the people who warn against water who also rave about the benefits of steaming the face. What is steam but vaporized hot water?

In fact, steaming is an excellent way to "deep cleanse" your skin, whether it be dry, oily, or average. Simply bend over the sink, drape a towel over your head and the basin,

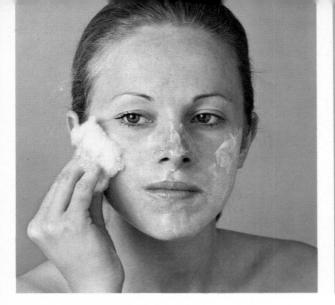

Above: when you use your cleansing lotions to fully remove your make-up, be sure to allow a few minutes to penetrate before wiping it off.

Below: steaming your skin is a luxurious way to give it a thorough cleansing—and it leaves you feeling fresh and wide-awake all over your face.

and turn on the hot water. Presto! You have a home sauna that does wonders for your skin. A word of caution, however: a really dry complexion gets enough steam during baths and showers without extra vaporizing.

For any woman with dry skin, the frequent use of a moisturizer, preferably one designed especially for dry skin, is absolutely essential. Because her skin is not producing enough natural lubricants, it positively cries out for protection. So heed its call. Surprisingly enough, it is estimated that no fewer than three out of every five adult women have dry skin. There are many reasons for this. First, of course, the glands that feed the skin have a natural tendency to slow down as we get older, producing less and less oil. Secondly we ourselves do a great deal to speed up the drying process: we use hard water, we live in centrally-heated houses, we smoke and drink, and we have a positive fetish about suntanning.

The drying effects of hard water and central heating are obvious, but what about cigarettes? When you surround your face in a perpetual cloud of smoke, you are drying the surface of your skin in the same way as the man who turns herrings into kippers by smoking them. More mysteriously, the inhalation of cigarette smoke seems to dry the skin from the inside as well—exactly how, no one knows, but the fact that smokers get wrinkles sooner than nonsmokers is a proven medical fact.

A similar principle applies in the case of alcohol. Astringents, which are alcohol-based, work by drying the skin from the outside. Alcohol is a dehydrator, whether you apply it or imbibe it, and the regular consumption of scotch and gin can be just as damaging to dry skin as the reckless use of astringents. So try to stick to beer and wine. Their alcohol content is lower, and their insidious drying effects much less.

Now, what about the harmful effects of the sun? We all know how important it is to avoid the pain and discomfort of sunburn, whether it be the result of too many hours in the sun, or the improper use of a sun lamp.

No one is more conscious of this than the woman with fair skin, which burns to a crisp in a few short minutes if she doesn't coat herself with oils. The fair-complexioned aren't the only ones in danger, though. No matter what her complexion, a woman can do herself irreparable harm by carrying on a lifelong love affair with the sun.

The simple fact of the matter is that tanning the skin tends to dry and thicken it, to rob it of its natural plasticity, and to encourage it to age and wrinkle faster than it would ordinarily. Sounds bad, doesn't it? Alas, it's all too true. As one dermatologist puts it: "Sunbathing sessions are skin-aging sessions."

So, whether you be fair or dark, it's best to regard the sun as a potential enemy. Don't expose yourself to the sun's rays for long periods, especially on overcast or windy days, even after you've acquired a moderate tan. Coat yourself liberally and frequently with a protective lotion, cream, or gel. Before you do, read the label carefully. Unless it states clearly and unequivocally that it's designed to block out the sun's rays, rather than merely keep the skin moist, it simply won't protect you. By the way, if you've read a few frightening articles about the sun causing skin cancer, you can relax a little. It happens only rarely, and only to a small fraction of lifetime sun worshipers. But why take any chances? Forewarned is forearmed, however slight the risk.

Basically, of course, it's almost impossible to resist the summertime pressure to acquire a tan as quick as you can. But remember that you can always have a tan—simply and safely—by using one of the many tanning preparations now on the market. The so-called "tanners" work by forming a chemical bond with the keratin in your skin, and last for weeks. The "bronzers" are more like a cosmetic. They don't last as long, but they give a marvelously even color to the skin.

After all this talk about things that can dry out your skin, what can you do to nourish and lubricate it? There are now dozens of products available to help you do

Above: both alcohol and cigarettes are hard on your skin, contributing to the aging process by drying out natural oils.

Right: sunbathing in the hot sun—and having a deep tan to show for it—is an annual treat for many of us. But the sun is not kind to skin, and even the action of tanning is the skin's mechanism to protect itself from further damage. To keep your skin as youthful as possible, treat the sun respectfully and don't let your sunbathing period last for hours.

just that. They go by all kinds of names: skin foods, night creams, antiwrinkle creams, vitamin creams, and hormone creams. Various special claims are made for each of these preparations, but you'll notice that the word "cream" appears in almost every one of them. In fact, it's the creamy ingredient, usually a fairly rich oil, in all of them that benefits your skin. Although it cannot take the place of your own natural oils, it can supplement them. In fact, if used regularly, a good cream will help to keep dry skin smooth and supple.

There is one thing that must be borne in mind when using any nourishing cream. Used too heavily, it can clog the pores and leave your eyes a bit puffy. So it's best to apply it a half-hour, or so before going to bed. Massage it gently into your skin, wait about 15 minutes, then blot off the excess with a tissue. By the time you go to bed, the cream will have been absorbed—and you won't wake up looking soggy.

One thing we haven't looked at yet is blemishes and how to deal with them. These can happen to anyone, though they do tend to be more of a problem for those with oily skin. They appear for all kinds of reasons: improper cleansing, lack of sleep, lack of exercise, poor diet, even anxiety.

Acne, of course, is a special problem all on its own, and many of us have experienced its scourge during our teenage years and/or young adulthood. "Why," many a young woman has asked, "do I still have acne now that I'm over 21?" For the very same reason she had it as a teenager: because, during her early childbearing years, the hormones responsible for the overproduction of oil on her skin have not yet settled down. Her only consolation is to know that eventually the hormones will regulate themselves better— and then, with her naturally more oily skin, she will remain wrinkle-free far longer than the girl whose drier skin kept her from ever having acne in the first place.

If you are still an acne sufferer at present, don't give up hope and hide away. The first thing to do—if you haven't done it already— is to see a dermatologist. He may prescribe some pills, a special fat-free diet, medicated lotions, or sun lamp treatments. But whatever he prescribes, he will undoubtedly urge you to keep your face scrupulously clean. Your skin can tolerate a somewhat strong soap, and frequent washings will help keep the pores free and clear while the medications are doing their good work.

Even if you don't have acne, but are plagued by the occasional blackhead or whitehead—what do you do about your blemishes? Blackheads are clogged oil ducts that have turned dark through contact with the air. It's best not to squeeze them, because they can all too easily become infected. Instead, try steaming your face, then washing the area thoroughly with soap and water. Repeat the process, three times a day if necessary, until you get results. Unless the blackheads are fiendishly stubborn, this method will oust them in a few days' time.

Whiteheads are closed cysts under the skin. They usually result from improper cleansing or poor diet. Unlike blackheads, they don't respond well to soap and water. If you find you've got quite a few and they worry you, make an appointment with a dermatologist. He and he alone can open them up safely.

Below: if the soft down on your upper lip is a little too dark, try using a mild bleaching solution to lighten it.

Below: be sure that the tweezers you use for eyebrow plucking have smooth flat ends, and that you clean them in alcohol before plucking.

If, however, you're troubled by the occasional white-topped pimple, you can open it up yourself—but only after it has come to a head. Sterilize a needle and gently prick the top. Then, very gently, press or squeeze the area on either side with a tissue, until only clear blood comes out. Finally, dab it with an antiseptic to help it heal.

There are two other kinds of "blemishes" many of us worry about: moles and facial hair. Moles are something only an expert can advise you about. As a general rule, however, it's wise to avoid plucking hairs from them or rubbing them vigorously when you wash your face. The potentially cancerous mole is extremely rare, but it's always best to be careful.

When it comes to removing facial hair, you

Making up a face mask yourself is simple and fun—and you can be sure it's perfectly suited to your own kind of skin.

Right: this mask is best for clear dry skin. The recipe is quick and easy:
Yolk of 1 egg
1 teaspoonful of honey
1 teaspoonful of olive oil
Mix ingredients and apply to face and neck. Rinse off after 10-15 minutes. Caution—never use this mask if you have any eruptions on your skin.

have a wide assortment of swift and efficient methods to choose from. Chemical, wax, and abrasive depilatories are all discussed in Chapter 5, because they each work as well on large areas of your body as they do on small, well-defined ones.

If your problem is simply a downy moustache, the best method is bleaching, using an ounce of beautician's peroxide to which you have added 20 drops of ammonia. Leave it on just long enough to bleach the

hair, then rinse it off with cool fresh water.

If it's simply extra hairy eyebrows that bother you, the best solution is plucking. Use a good pair of tweezers that end in a flat surface rather than in two sharp points. Dip the tweezers in alcohol and pull out the unwanted hairs quickly, firmly, and at the same angle at which they grow. Then cleanse the brows well with antiseptic.

If you're really worried about facial hair, your best bet is electrolysis, the most delicate

Left: if your skin tends to be oily, an astringent mask like the white one shown here is more likely to help your skin along.

Juice of half a lemon
White of 1 egg
Mix to a paste with light carbonate of magnesium, which you get from the drugstore. Apply to face and neck, but be sure to keep the area around your eyes free, as shown here. Rinse the mask off with warm water after about 10 or 15 minutes.

and permanent method of hair removal. But it must be done by an expert, and several sessions may be required to achieve the results you want. At each session, the operator will insert a tiny needle into selected hair follicles. The current that passes through the needle instantly destroys the roots. One reason why it takes several sessions is that too intensive a treatment of any confined area might cause undue inflammation. Another reason is that some of the hair follicles may be going through a "resting phase," only to emerge later on. The great advantage of electrolysis is that it is not only permanent, but also selective. It doesn't remove the fine down that is a natural and characteristic part of the skin.

Getting back to general face care, there is something all of us can do that is both a treat and a treatment. That something is the face mask. There are all sorts of face pack preparations on the market, designed to do all

Making faces gives your face the regular exercise it needs and probably isn't getting ordinarily. This face exercises a muscle that helps open your mouth. As gravity does most of that job, it can get lax and contribute to a pudgy double chin.

A strong pucker with your mouth open makes you look a bit goony. But, even if you have to laugh at yourself afterward, you've done your face a good turn by using the muscles at the corners of your mouth, which will help keep the skin smooth.

manner of things—from cleansing, to toning and stimulating, to lubricating your skin. It's much more fun to make your own, though, and, as you can see from the pictures and recipes on the previous page, it's the type of skin you have that decides which concoction you're going to treat yourself to.

How often should you give yourself this kind of facial? Again, it depends entirely on your skin type and, of course, on how often you feel like doing it. In general, however, dry skin reacts best to a once-a-week facial of the lubricating type, and oily skin to a twice-weekly facial of the toning and freshening type. Either one is left on the face for 10 to 15

minutes, and rinsed off with warm, then cool, water.

No discussion of face care would be complete without mentioning the marvelous benefits of facial massage and exercise. Both of them can, and should, be a standard feature of your daily self-care program.

Every time you cleanse your face or apply make-up, remember to use gentle, upward, circular movements. And be especially kind to the delicate area just under your eyes. Fifty tiny little taps under each eye every day helps tone up this very sensitive tissue.

As for facial exercises, we've illustrated a few of the best ones for you on these pages.

Another pucker, this time the more usual almost-closed one, as if you were about to whistle. Now you're using the lower lip muscles, which seldom get exercise—and help prevent formation of heavy grooves running from corners of the mouth to chin.

Try imitating the wiseacre who talks from the corner of his mouth, and then stretch your mouth open in that position, twisting your head to the side at the same time. This exercises the heavy neck muscle and helps keep your neck unwrinkled.

They each have a specific purpose, and, although funny looking in themselves, can do wonders to keep your facial muscles supple and resilient. Do them in front of the mirror. You'll get a kick out of watching yourself, and an even bigger kick out of seeing the results later on.

Finally, there are two vitally important things to remember about face care. First, whatever you do, you must do it regularly. The occasional crash program won't do you any good if you're going to drop the whole thing and neglect your skin for long intervals. Start a "happy face" program and keep at it until, to miss out any part of it would make you feel positively cheated.

The second point to remember is that your face is a living, ever-changing part of the total you. As your expression reflects your state of mind, so your skin reflects your state of health. It is a clear barometer of how well you eat, sleep, and exercise—even of what medicines you're taking. It is also affected by changes in the weather, and by alterations in your own glandular output. Keep a careful watch on your complexion, and always be prepared to adapt your program to suit its changing needs. You have only one face, dear to all who love you. It's up to you to take care of it.

1

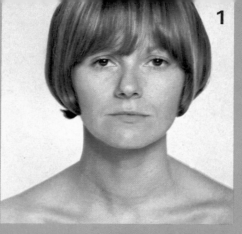

2

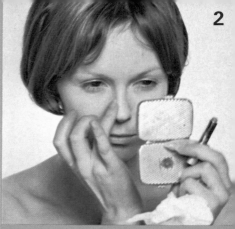

4

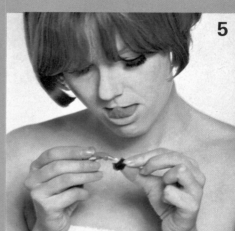

5

7

8

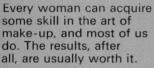

Every woman can acquire some skill in the art of make-up, and most of us do. The results, after all, are usually worth it.

The making of a beauty.
1. Clean face, ready to go.
2. Over a foundation base, she shades the sides of her nose with dark powder.
3. An over-all powder with a swansdown puff.
4. Eyes defined with liner.
5. False eyelashes cut to shape and adhesive applied
6. Mascara blends the false lashes with the real.
7. Powdered rouge goes high on the cheekbones.
8. A darker lipstick for the top lip than bottom.
9. Long blond hairpiece gets brushed vigorously.
10. Hairpiece is pinned carefully into position. The final result: it took 20 minutes to achieve— and it will take another 20 to remove it all.

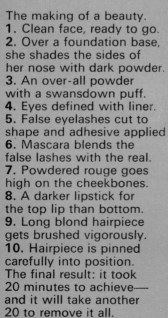

9

10

The Lovely Art of Making Up

3

A young man in love gazes adoringly at his sweetheart, sighs, and whispers, "Your eyes are like stars. What makes them so beautiful?" "Well," she says, irresistibly moved to laughter by the very solemn look on his face, "if you really want to know, it's mascara!"

This little interchange, taken from an Indian movie of the 1950's, speaks volumes about the art of make-up. Though most women wouldn't give away their secrets so easily, they do want to provoke wonder and admiration. And why not? The true magic of make-up (as women everywhere have discovered) is that it really can enhance your looks.

Women began experimenting with cosmetics long before the invention of the looking glass—way back when they had only pools of water or squares of polished metal to see themselves in. Often, too, it wasn't only the women who took pleasure in paints and powders. Among many American Indian tribes, it was customary for the men to paint their faces and bodies even when they weren't on the warpath. And in Africa and the South Pacific, both sexes used paints, tatoos, and even painfully carved-in designs to decorate their skin.

Every age and culture has made its own unique contribution to the cosmetic scene. For sheer sophistication, though, perhaps none has ever topped the techniques devised by the ancient Egyptians. One has only to look at the lovely face of Queen Nefertiti to see how artfully they were using make-up as early as 1400 B.C.

Nefertiti's make-up palette included a

JOAN CRAWFORD

MARILYN
MONROE

Cosmetics styles vary as identifiably as the clothes we wear. Jean Harlow, Rita Hayworth, Joan Crawford, and Marilyn Monroe are each datable by their make-up (that's often because so many others took up their originally individual styles). The look of today is simpler to achieve as cosmetics become more varied and easier to use skillfully.

lush green eyeshadow, in the form of a paste made from malachite, as well as a lustrous dark eyeliner called galena, an early form of the kohl later used by the beauties of India. She shaped her eyebrows with black antimony powder, and rouged her lips and cheeks with a rosy red pigment called ocher. The total effect was both worldly and vibrant. No wonder we all took it up again after Elizabeth Taylor's film portrayal of Cleopatra, another legendary lady of the Nile.

The Greeks and Romans adopted many of the Egyptian cosmetics, while far away in the East, the Japanese were perfecting the highly elaborate make-up techniques that are still used today by Japan's delicate geisha girls.

In our own culture, we have passed through many weird and wonderful phases in the use of cosmetics. Some of the ingredients once used were almost unbelievably dangerous. One has only to think of the days, which lasted from Tudor times until the end of the 18th century, when women powdered their faces, necks, and bosoms with white lead, a substance which, because it contained arsenic, actually killed several well-known actresses and aristocratic ladies.

Another rather bizarre cosmetic was sublimate of mercury which, although it gave the complexion a bright, translucent look, also tended to corrode the flesh little by little. Yet another tricky beauty gimmick— this one used by the ladies of the 19th century—was belladonna, a form of liquid opium guaranteed to make your eyes fashionably languid and misty—albeit somewhat

out of focus—if you put enough of it into them.

Our attitudes toward cosmetics have undergone sweeping changes since the beginning of this century, when, as in certain other periods of Western history, there was a distinct feeling that make-up was not worn by "nice" women. Once respectable women did take to wearing make-up—and they began doing so full throttle in the "Roaring Twenties"—the modern cosmetics industries really got under way.

There was a slight slump during World War II. Women didn't stop wearing make-up by any means, but research and development came to a relative halt. Postwar, however, the cosmetic companies unleashed a positive flood of new products, and ever since, we have been benefiting from the work of dedicated experts who, with the watchful eye of the U.S. Food and Drug Administration ever upon them, have provided us with a wonderful range of safe cosmetics.

It gives you pause for thought, doesn't it, this flashback through the history of make-up? If nothing else, it proves that we belong to a time-honored sisterhood that stretches far back into the mists of time, and away to the very ends of the earth. The universal attraction of make-up also explains why, at the very height of the "natural look," we have found ourselves buying and using just

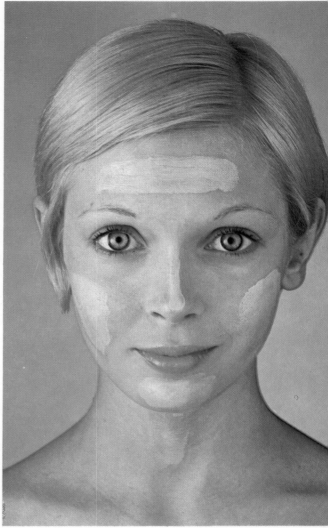

as much make-up as ever. We're not to be robbed of our pleasure in using cosmetics, even when it involves what may well be the most complicated make-up techniques of all time. The best "natural look"—as you've probably discovered—is the result of the subtlest and most painstaking artistry. It's a lovely look, but hardly less time-consuming than the "Cleopatra look" that preceded it, or the bright, glamour girl look that's on the way.

Your foundation is the base for all the rest of the make-up you apply. The color and type you choose is intimately allied to the kind of skin you have. A medicated foundation can treat skin as well as cover blemishes. A foundation combined with moisturizers can be a day-long blessing to the girl with dry skin—and if you have fair skin but must be out in the sun, try a foundation with a built-in sun filter to keep you pale and pretty.

44

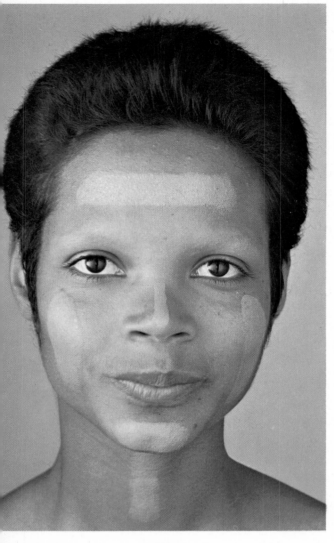

So on to the nitty-gritty: the basic rules to follow when making up your face. For, whichever way the fashion pendulum swings, be it bright or muted, there are rules to follow if you want to get the best results and be kind to your skin at the same time.

The most important rule, of course, is to start with an absolutely clean skin—toned up with freshener if your complexion is oily—and moisturized, whatever your skin type. This isn't extravagance. Moisturizer not only makes the next coat of make-up glide on more smoothly, but it also gives your skin extra protection against the pollutants in the air. There are some excellent moisturizers that can be worn under make-up. A few are even slightly tinted to blend with your foundation.

Foundation is just what the name implies: the groundwork for every other bit of make-up you apply. Whether matte or plain, it's designed to do a surprising number of things, from supplying basic color and texture, to masking tiny blemishes, to providing a good base for lipstick, eyeshadow, and blushers.

Choose your foundation color carefully. It shouldn't differ too much from your own natural skin tone. If your skin is sallow (a bit on the yellowish side), or if it has that deathly pallor that suggests you've just stepped out of a sick-bed, choose a peachy-pink shade. If you have an olive complexion, choose beige or

Below each girl is pictured the range of foundation colors for different complexions of white and black skin. You'll probably discover that, in addition to your basic color, you can mix and match one or two others according to your mood. Remember, though, that your foundation color should not differ markedly from your own skin tone. The point is not to give yourself a whole new complexion, but to add bloom and finish to the one you have.

tan. If your skin is black (and there are over 40 different shades of black skin), you may want to choose two foundations, a dark one for around your eyes, forehead, nose, and chin, and a lighter one to highlight your cheekbones.

Foundations come in all kinds of forms: bottled liquids and creams, sticks (called "slickers"), gels in tubes, cakes (which require a sponge to apply), even aerosol foams. They all give excellent coverage, but

Blushers are an easy way to bring a quick glow to your complexion. They come in many forms, but all should be applied over the fuller part of the cheek. See opposite page for hints on special face shapes.

a word to the wise: if your skin is oily, avoid the creams, and if your skin is dry, stay away from the cakes and gels, which tend to have a tightening effect.

Assuming that you've chosen your foundation, what's the best way to apply it? First of all, clear the field of action by pinning your hair up and away from your face and neck. Make sure the light you're working in is strong and clear. Then, put a bit of the foundation on your fingertips and, using long, gentle strokes, massage it into one section of your face at a time: cheeks, eye area, nose, forehead, chin, neck—even ears, if you wear your hair up. Apply it as sparingly as you can, and be sure to blend it in evenly. There's nothing worse than a telltale demarcation line that shows exactly where art and nature meet. Finally, blot off any excess foundation with a tissue.

Now that the base coat is on, you're ready to add special color and focus to individual features. Many beauty experts recommend contouring—the shading and highlighting of special areas of the face to enhance basic bone structure. Without doubt, skillful contouring can do wonders to flatter your face, but it must be done with the utmost subtlety, or you'll find yourself looking like a patchwork quilt. We've included some illustrations to serve as guidelines on how to use shaders and highlighters to shape and flatter different kinds of faces.

Whether or not you contour your face, you'll undoubtedly want to add a touch of color over your cheekbones to accentuate them and give your face a healthy bloom. The most popular form of rouge these days is the blush-on, applied with a soft, fluffy brush. But you may prefer one of the creamy rouges, which come in the form of gels, sticks, and liquids. Whichever you choose, bear in mind that clear red is best for black skins, peachy-beige for olive or sallow skins,

46

and rosy-pink for lighter skins.

Now, your eyes. They are your most vital feature, for they not only mirror your feelings, but give sparkle and focus to your entire face. They are also the feature others notice first. So, whatever their shape or hue, they deserve very special attention.

Let's begin with eyeshadow. Matte or shiny, it comes in a variety of forms: sticks, gels, creams, brush-on powders, and paint-box cakes. The last two are especially good if you have very deep-set eyes because they adhere well and won't cake up in the recess of the eyelid. As always, if your skin is dry, it's best to be kind to it and use a creamy shadow, and set it afterwards with a light dusting of translucent powder.

There's a remarkable range of eyeshadow colors to choose from today—everything from blue and beige, to gray and green, to lavender and plum. Gone are the days when you had to match your shadow to the color of your eyes. Experiment a little. You'd be surprised at the difference a subtle new shade can make.

The trick to remember when applying eyeshadow is to blend it into your skin, applying it more intensely to the eyelid itself, and then carefully shading it into the area above. Go easy—it shouldn't extend farther than the outer tip of the eyebrow. Special hints on how to use shadow to make your eyes look larger or farther apart, more or less prominent, are illustrated above. If you use a highlighter—usually found in shades of beige or cream—to draw attention to your eyes, use it sparingly, and only on the prominent bone just under your eyebrow.

Speaking of eyebrows, now is the time to do them—while your eye-shadow is drying. Use a soft pencil in a color just a shade deeper than your hair, and apply it with short, feathery strokes. As a general rule of thumb, the higher your forehead, the higher should be the top of the arch, while the closer your eyes are set, the father out you should extend the brow line. After darkening your brows, brush-blend them with a fine, dry brush to soften the line.

The oval face is the classic "perfect" shape: try experimenting with rouge winging from the point of the cheekbone, as here, for new interest.

With a pear-shaped face, widen the forehead by using a lighter tone at the sides. Soften jawline with a darker shadow under both cheekbones.

For a square face, use rouge from the cheek-bone toward the ears, and a darker foundation below, toward the jaw.

A heart-shaped face can have rouge high on the cheeks to soften width. Try a darker foundation to widen the chin subtly.

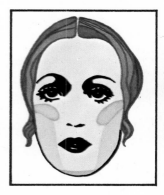

An oblong face can be widened with pale rouge on the cheekbones, fading out to the ears. Then blend in contour rouge down toward the chin.

With a round face, suck in your cheeks and apply rouge to the hollows. Use a darker foundation to shade around the jaw and just under the chin.

47

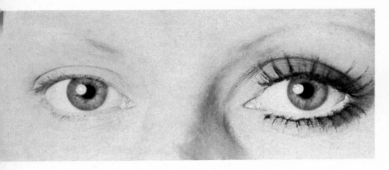

Now you're ready to apply mascara to darken and thicken your eyelashes. The roll-on types are especially easy to use, but a little difficult to remove at night. The block types, applied with a damp brush, are easier to get off, but less moisture proof. So if you're going through a weepy phase, better use a roll-on. Whichever type you use, brush on with upward, outward strokes and, if you're going to apply a second coat, let the first one dry before doing so.

False eyelashes are great, particularly if your own are very fine or sparse. But fake "sweepers" should look as natural as possible. They usually need trimming to make them exactly right for you. When you trim them, do it a bit unevenly—the straight-across look is anything but natural. If you're just beginning to use them, follow the instructions on the package very carefully. You'll probably need a lot of practice, too, for as anyone who wears them will tell you, getting them on takes steady hands and a lot of patience.

By the way, it's best to put on false eye-

Eye make-up is a fascinatingly complex art, which can change the whole appearance of your face. Above left: undefined eyes can grow big and lovely with a bright blue shadow smudged around the eye, and two coats of black mascara on the eyelashes. Above center: sallow skin can be brightened by a paprika-red eye shadow, used with black mascara. Above right: when you do experiment with the new colors, be sure to stick to a single one (or two tones of the same shade) or you'll look like a clown. Here yellow and greenish-yellow work well.

lashes before you apply mascara. That way, you can use the mascara to blend your own eyelashes with the false ones, thus avoiding the "double layer" effect.

The last step in making up your eyes should be eyeliner. Whatever the color—be it gray, brown, blue, or black—you'll find it comes in three forms: pencil, paint-box cake, or bottled liquid, the latter two applied with a brush. All three are good, although, with the cake type, it's best to powder over your eyeshadow first to avoid smearing. Keeping as close to the edge of the eyelid as you can, start from the inner corner of your eye—or a bit farther along if your eyes are close-set—

For deep-set eyes, use a pale shadow of white highlighter on the lids. Keep the liner thin and light.

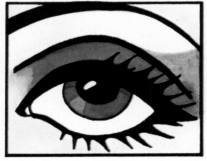

For prominent eyes, use a pale neutral shadow on the lid and define the socket with a brown line.

For small eyes, use highlighter from the inner corner to the brow. Use a soft liner under the eye.

Above: avoid hardness by blending eye liner into eye shadow with a damp brush. Shade the colors while still wet. Right: the big-eyed look comes from three shades of green: mid-blue-green on the lid, paler green on the socket, palest green up to the eyebrow.

and draw out to, or just beyond, the outer corner. If you're wearing false eyelashes, eyeliner has a fringe benefit in that it can cover any trace of eyelid still showing beneath the lashes.

If, when you've finished putting on your eye make-up, you find that late-night circles under your eyes are detracting from the total effect, you can use a concealer. These come in shades of clear red for black skin, cream or beige for white or olive skin. They must be used sparingly, and blended with great care into your skin, or they will point up the very circles you're trying to hide.

A special hint here to all those who wear glasses. You can be a little more liberal in your use of eyeshadow, mascara, and liner. A bit more of these will give your eyes that extra definition and enhancement they need. Also—and you probably know this already— you'll want to get right up close to the mirror if you're nearsighted, or stand back a bit if you're farsighted, while you apply your make-up. Then put on your glasses and study the finished effect to make sure you've got it just the way you want it.

Now is the moment to decide whether you need powder. You do if your make-up has taken on a shine on nose, chin or forehead. A loose, translucent powder is the best kind

Widen close-set eyes with pale shadow on the inner half of the lids and use darker shadow on the outer.

For round eyes, use a colorful shadow diagonally from inner corner to brow. Use liner to lengthen eye.

Falling eyes need shadow winging up and out. Keep the liner thin, and tilted upward at the outer edge.

49

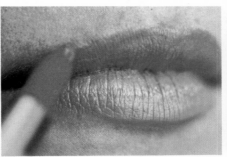
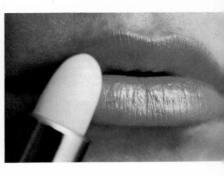

To reduce lips, pencil inside natural line, and use two tones of lipstick.

For a movie star pout, outline with red and fill in pale, glossy lipstick.

A gloss over your regular lipstick gives a shiny, moist appeal to your lips.

to use if you're putting on your make-up at home. Compressed, or compact, powders are fine for touching up your make-up during the day, but they shouldn't be used too often because they tend to add unwanted color.

The very last step in making up is, of course, lipstick. Again, there's an almost unlimited range of colors available, and what you choose depends entirely on what looks best on you. In applying lipstick, it sometimes helps to first outline your lips in color with a fine brush. There are also a couple of tricks you can use to alter the shape of your lips subtly. For example, you can make them appear fuller by dabbing a bit of creamy beige eyeshadow on the middle of your lower lip. Or, to make full lips look a trifle thinner, you can use a slightly darker shade of lipstick on the lower lip.

Lip glossers and slickers give an added sheen to the lips. You can either put them directly on your lips, for a heightened natural look, or stroke them on over your lipstick. A great many lipsticks today contain their own slicks and moisturizers, which not only gloss the lips, but also protect them from chapping.

If you're one of the many women who find that lipstick colors betray them by turning excessively dark or slightly bluish after a few minutes, don't give up hope. The first thing to do is to test every lipstick before buying it. Apply it to the padded tips of your fingers, where the pigmentation of the skin is closest to that on your lips. This is a dandy way to

test as many as ten lipsticks at once. Wait a full five minutes. If, after that time, the color you want remains true, you can count on it to stay true on your lips. If all else fails, there are special yellow lipsticks you can buy to wear under pinker shades. These contain less eosin, the staining ingredient that darkens as it reacts with the chemicals in your skin.

This is a good point at which to mention the possibility of developing an adverse reaction to any of your cosmetics. All make-up contains a wide variety of ingredients, both natural and man-made. And all of them, be they as simple as beeswax and lanolin, or as complex as aryl-sulphonamide formaldehyde, are potential irritants to certain skins. Obviously, the cosmetic manufacturers would be crazy to produce and market any make-up that had a marked tendency to produce irritation. They'd be out of business in a hurry if they did. Moreover, in recent years, many cosmetic companies have increasingly concerned themselves with the purity of their products, even vying with one another to simplify and pare down the ingredients in their formulas to create what they call hypoallergenic make-ups.

Basically, there is no such thing as a *completely* nonallergenic cosmetic. Every substance under the sun has the potential to cause an allergic reaction in someone. As with hay fever, the allergy can develop overnight, and a woman who has used the same make-up year in and year out with no ill effects may suddenly find that one of her old standbys is

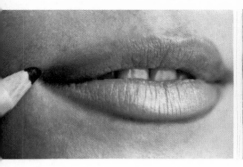

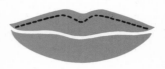

Reshape your lips with a pink lip pencil or a brown eyebrow pencil. For a fuller top lip, make a new line outside the lip and fill in with lipstick.

For lusher lips, outline outside lip line with brown. Fill in lipstick.

For a clearer edge, outline with brush and fill in with the same color.

You can make a large mouth seem smaller by drawing a fine line just inside your natural line and then filling in the new shape with lipstick.

For any mouth reshaping, start with foundation spread over your lips. Then you can widen a thin lower lip to match the top one, and fill in.

If your mouth is unevenly shaped, reshape the edge to balance the good side with your pencil, and fill in only the new shape with lipstick.

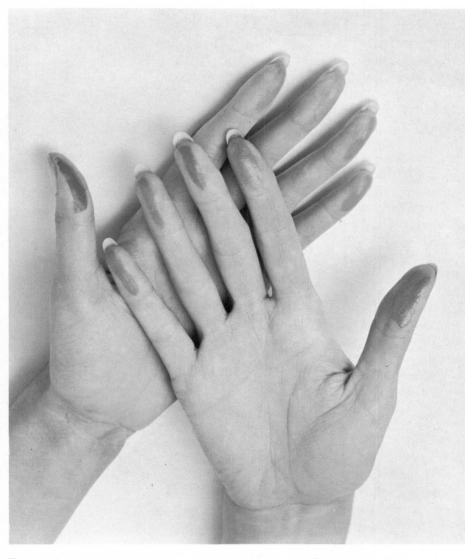

Try out lipstick colors before you buy, and use your fingers to test them. Your fingertips are handy—and closest to the natural color of your lips.

If your top lip protrudes over the bottom one, you can emphasize the bottom lip by widening it a little. Turn up the drooping curves of the top lip.

Changing your style of make-up for daytime, night-time, or the seasons can put you in a better mood.
Right: a fresh natural day look—brown-toned lip-stick and only a little make-up for the eyes.
Below: a more elaborate day look, with darker foundation and eyeshadow keyed to bright clothes.
Far right: an elegant look for the evening. A clear but darker color for lips, smoky gray eye shadow.

beginning to cause irritation. Thankfully, there are hundreds of different brands and products to choose from, and if, for some reason, you find that a particular one doesn't agree with your skin, the solution is simply to try another, perhaps a hypoallergenic one.

You may have been wondering whether or not there is any real difference between the expensive and inexpensive brands of make-up on the market. Well, there is and there isn't. The sheer pressure of competition has produced a fairly even level of improvement throughout the cosmetic industry, whatever the cost of the specific product. It is also true that the companies that produce the higher priced items put more research—and sooner—into developing their products than their competitors. They also tend to put their cosmetics in more attractive, and convenient, containers, and sometimes even include finer ingredients.

The real difference between the high and low priced make-ups, however, is a psychological one. As always, beauty lies not only in the eye of the beholder. If it makes you feel special—luxurious and pampered—to pay more for your make-up, and if, having done so, you get more fun out of using it, do it.

A final word about you and your make-up. Never restrict yourself to just one "look." Vary your techniques to suit your mood, your activities, the time of day, even the seasons. One of the best things about make-up is that it's not only flexible, but it's also entirely at your command. Better still, by flattering your looks, it enhances your self-image. A well made up face can make you feel less of a drudge while you're cleaning the house, and more of a princess when, on a special night out, you want to shine forth at your most beautiful.

Locks and Tresses, Plain and Fancy

4

Have you ever read a novel in which the author didn't describe the heroine's crowning glory? Probably not. Be it raven, chestnut, red, or gold, there's always something curiously revealing about the style and texture of her hair. Just knowing that it is "thick as a rope" or "fine as cornsilk," "a mass of curls" or "a free-flowing mane," somehow gives us a vivid picture of her.

Not surprisingly, the same is true in life. A woman's hair plays a vital role in the total impression she creates. Why? Partly, of course, for the simple reason that it frames and sets off her face, but also because, in some deeper and more basic way, it serves as an outward symbol of her whole being. A lustrous, well-cared-for head of hair can speak as eloquently about her capacity for living as the expression on her face and the way she carries herself.

We all know that healthy hair makes for beautiful hair. But we sometimes forget that healthy hair is part and parcel of a healthy body. Your hair, like your skin, is a living, breathing part of the total you. And it's just as much affected by your ups and downs. The amazing thing is how quickly it will respond to even the slightest bit of extra care.

To meet the special needs of your hair, it helps to understand the way it grows and what affects it. This brings us to the heart—or more precisely, to the *root*—of the matter. For it is in its roots, or follicles, that the

secrets of hair lie. Each root is a miniature factory, in which hair is made, nourished, and kept lubricated through a link-up with the oil glands under the skin.

By the way, if your hair tends to be extra oily, it's because this network of tiny oil glands is working overtime. If, on the other hand, your problem is very dry and brittle hair, it's because the oil glands are not working hard enough.

Each hair is made of keratin, a type of protein, and grows out straight or curly depending on the inner structure of its root. If the root is smooth inside, the hair shaft will come out round and straight. If the root is somewhat uneven, the hair will be more oval, a bit twisted, and more likely to end in a curl.

Whether you have a mop of short curls or long, straight locks, you have between 90,000 and 140,000 individual hairs on your head. That's roughly 1,000 per square inch. More surprising still, if all their growing power were put into a single hair, it would grow at the breakneck speed of 60 miles an hour. This gives you some idea of the determined industry of those little follicles. On average, hair grows at the rate of about a half-inch per month, though this tends to slow up as we get older. It also seems to grow faster by day than by night, and faster during warm weather.

The life span of a single hair can be as short as a few months or as long as several years. What makes it fall out? Each hair has its own cycle of growth and decline, a period of vigorous growth being followed by a "resting phase," which ends in its falling out and being replaced by a new hair. Fortunately, they don't all go through this

Hair has always had a wide range of significance—sexual, social, symbolic. For a woman herself, her hair is simply one of the most potent weapons in her beauty armory. All the more reason for her to spend time and loving care on her "crowning glory."

Left: moderate brushing is good for any type of hair. It removes the dust and grit picked up from the air, and helps stimulate the scalp. But if your hair is oily, brushing will also help to stimulate the oil production—so take it easy on the amount of hair brushing you do.

process at the same time. It's perfectly natural to lose a certain number of hairs every day, but if you find yourself suddenly losing more than usual, you should consult a tricologist. It may be that you're simply rundown, or that you're suffering from a bad case of dandruff, which tends to block the roots. It may also be that you've got the beginnings of a minor scalp condition, which needs to be treated with special medications.

Why is it that some women can grow their hair down to their waists or below, while others find that it simply refuses to grow beyond their shoulder blades? The lucky ones have hair that combines a quick rate of growth with a relatively long life span. They are also probably fairly young, in good health, and take good care of their hair.

Does cutting your hair make it grow faster? No, but it certainly gives the impression that it does. The fact is that hair gets impoverished as it moves farther away from its source of nourishment and lubrication. At the same time, the split ends are traveling upward. By cutting off the split and impoverished ends, you create the illusion of having thicker, healthier, and more vigorously growing hair at the bottom.

What makes hair turn gray? In fact, it doesn't turn gray, but white. What happens

Right: clean, fresh hair is an asset to any girl. The variety of shampoos on the market is truly amazing, so experiment until you can find the one that suits you and your hair. Even then, it's a good idea to keep an open mind about trying a new one: remember, hair changes with your state of health, and if you've been ill or rundown, it may need a bit of extra pampering.

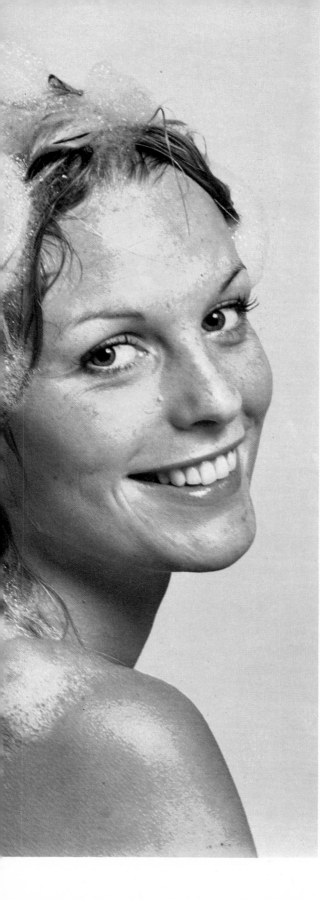

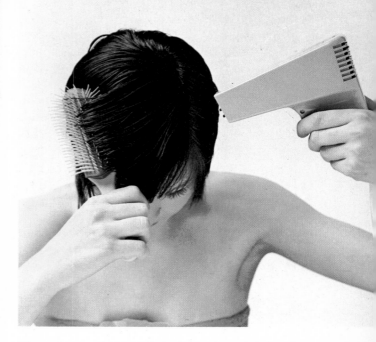

The way you dry your hair depends mainly on the hairstyle you wear. If it's straight, you may find that blowing it dry gives the slight guidance it needs. If you need to set it, a hood or salon-type drier will do a much more efficient job.

is that the colored section of the hair shaft stops producing pigment, and fills up with colorless air bubbles. Because the white hairs are mixed in with the colored ones, the overall effect is gray. People lose their natural hair color at various ages, and with varying degrees of change in hair texture. If hair turns white at an early age, usually due to hereditary factors, the white strands may be coarser than the rest. When hair turns gray slowly, over the course of many years, the texture usually changes very little.

Now that you know a little more about the life and times of your hair, let's discuss how best to care for it. The first thing is to make sure you're feeding it properly—and that means from the inside. A high-protein diet, with lots of fruit and vegetables, is best for you, and best for your hair. Try to avoid fats and oils if your hair is naturally oily, but if it's dry, fats and oils will help to nourish it.

Something that's good for all hair types is brewers yeast tablets. They contain, in natural form, the Vitamin B complex that is so essential for healthy hair, skin, and nails. It's even been said that they can help curb balding, which might be a useful tip for your menfolk.

What about the "hundred strokes a day" routine our grannies used to practice? Such brushing is a great way to nourish the roots of your hair by improving the circulation— but do it only if your hair is strong, in good condition, and relatively dry. Brushing stimulates the oil glands at the same time that it stimulates the scalp. So it's obviously not a good idea if your hair is already oily. Simple exercising is just as good a way to give stimulation to your scalp.

It's always worth spending money on a good brush. Whether its bristles are natural or nylon, they should be finely finished; rough ones will only scratch the scalp and tear the hair. A nylon comb is all right, provided its teeth are rounded at the ends and joined to the bar in shallow scoops. The smoother the comb, the better for your hair.

Where both brush and comb are concerned, the best advice is, "Never a borrower nor a lender be." Also, be sure to wash them both thoroughly every time you wash your hair. Dunk them in a mild solution of ammonia and water to lift the grime. Then swish them around in warm soapy water, rinse well, and lay them out to dry. Put the brush upside down—not on a radiator.

Is it true that the more often you wash your hair the oilier it gets? Yes, insofar as washing stimulates the scalp and the oil glands just beneath it. Some hair is just naturally oily though, and requires more frequent washing. If yours is this type of hair, keep its style as simple as possible, and wash it as often as it needs it. What about special shampoos for oily hair? A few years ago, there were some whose action was so drastic, that they often damaged hair by over-cleaning it. Today, however, most shampoos are basically mild, whatever hair type they are designed for, and whether or not they contain special ingredients.

It's best to start your shampoo by brushing your hair forward from the nape and over the crown to smooth it out. Then wet it thoroughly with warm or lukewarm water (never, at any stage, use hot water), and work up a rich, soft lather with your shampoo. Be gentle; don't dig your fingers into your scalp or rub your hair as though it were a piece of clothing. Rinse well with warm, then cool water. To make sure all the shampoo is out of your hair, you can use lemon juice or vinegar–two tablespoons to a quart of water–in the last rinse. Lemon is best for blondes, vinegar for brunettes.

What about the use of a beaten egg or a bottle of beer during rinsing? Egg is a time-honored conditioner for dry hair, and does seem to make it more lustrous. Rinsing with beer gives the hair extra body. How? By mildly starching it, the way we used to starch our crinolines back in the 1950's. Beer—or, for that matter, lemonade or champagne—contains sugar, and it's that ingredient that makes hair feel crisper after rinsing with it. In fact, there are products on the market now that do much the same thing by coating the hair with clear plastics. Such products increase each hair's diameter, and give it more body.

To make your hair softer and easier to manage after washing, you can use a con-

Modern developments in wig making now give us practically as much versatility with a wig as with our own hair. These three pictures show the same woman with one wig, arranged differently. Right: the short straight layered look is an easy and flattering style.

Below left: try the allover curly look of finger-waved hair with waves framing your face. Below right: new wigs can be parted. This style is chin-length with soft bangs brushed over to one side of the face.

ditioner. There are three types available: those that come mixed in with your shampoo; those that come in the form of a cream-rinse for use just before a final, clear-water rinse; and those that are brushed into your hair after it's dry. All three contain nutriments, and act by smoothing down the tiny scales that form the outer layer of each hair. A conditioner can do your hair nothing but good, especially if it tends to be dry, or spiky.

When drying your hair, first wrap a towel around it to absorb the excess water. Then mop it dry; don't rub or wring it. Ideally, the tangles shouldn't be combed out right away, because your hair is at its most delicate while wet. However, if you're going to set it, you'll have to comb it out while it's still fairly wet. But be gentle. Don't, by any means, drag the comb through it fast and furiously.

Hairpieces can give you a quick and easy change of style—from the simple to the glamorous— or they can be used simply to add fullness to your own hair. The style on the left shows how a hairpiece gives a fuller look to a ponytail, while the hairpiece in the other style creates an elaborate coiffure for that special evening.

Hair tends to hold a curl longer if you put it up while it is still slightly damp, or moistened with a setting lotion. (The same principle applies to all natural fibers. A woolen dress, for example, holds its wrinkles if folded while damp.) The kind of roller you use is entirely up to you, but in general, the soft plastic ones are kindest to your hair. Obviously, you shouldn't tug the hair too hard as you roll it up, or dig fiercely into your scalp with clips or bobby pins. It's best, too, to allow some give between the scalp surface and the rolled-up hair, especially if you're going to sleep with a headful of pins and rollers.

To speed up the drying process, you can use a hand drier, or a portable hairdrying

cap. Never turn them up so high that they burn your ears or make the rollers too hot to handle. If this happens, you're baking your hair, and drying out the oils that give it natural luster. The same is true about sun bathing. A little sun is good for your hair, but too much will make it dry and brittle.

After your hair is dry and you've combed or brushed it into shape, you can use one of the many hair sprays now on the market to keep it in position and protect it from the effects of wind and moisture. Hair sprays work by forming a fine plastic film over the hair surface. The best kinds are the scentless ones; they don't clash with any other fragrance you may wish to use.

From time to time, we all find ourselves too busy to wash our hair, and this is when dry shampoos come in handy. They really do work wonders to absorb the excess oil that makes hair look dirty. Take it easy when you spray it on, and brush it out carefully, or you'll find you've swapped the oily look for the powdered wig effect.

Speaking of wigs, they too are a marvelous way to cover hair that's in need of washing, or simply to vary or glamourize your looks for a special occasion. The making of wigs, falls, and hairpieces has become a fine art, and, as the saying goes, "Every woman should have one"—if only to give her morale a boost from time to time when she needs a change. A word of caution, however: any wig should allow your scalp to breathe, and, if you're using a hairpiece, it should be pinned on firmly, but gently.

Now, what about the longer lasting ways of altering the shape of your hair, such as permanents and straighteners? Both of them work by affecting the molecular structure of your hair. In permanent waving or straightening, a strong chemical solution is applied to the hair first. This breaks the links between the keratin molecules in the hair shafts, and makes each hair more willing to do your bidding.

In the case of permanents, your hair is set,

Right: this basic cut, seen wet, will make the hair styles shown below

Far right: the set, with large rollers arranged in several straight rows. Notice that the bangs are set in pincurls.

Below left: from a side part, hair is brushed to one side, ends flipped, and split curl is added. Below: ends are flipped under. Some tiny braids, started at crown center, have their longish ends combed into rest of hair. Braids are secured by tying them up with thread. Below right: from an uneven center part, hair is brushed out, and waves pushed into place with fingers. Front waves frame face; ends are flipped. Below far right: hair is brushed straight down, a ring of overlapping bobby pins is made on the crown, loose hair is backcombed. Back hair is then rolled up and over, and pinned down. Side hair is flipped up, and brushed back in a soft sweep. Bangs are brushed lightly to the sides. Finally, a tiny wiglet of curls is attached to the crown.

in pin curls or rollers, and last of all, a neutralizing lotion is applied. The neutralizing lotion undoes the work of the breakdown chemical, and permits the keratin molecules to link up again in a new pattern. Voila! You have a permanent.

The same process is used in straightening, except that instead of curling the hair before applying the neutralizer, it is stretched. Possibly because in doing so the gaps between the keratin molecules are increased, it is a much trickier process, and should be done with the utmost care. Follow the instructions on the package to the letter, or better still, have it done at the hairdresser's.

Another, but less lasting way to relax curly hair is to run a warm comb, preferably an electric one, through it, after first coating your hair with oil. Heat has a way of making hair more willing to assume the shape you want it to have, at least temporarily. Again, it's essential to use care when using a heated comb to straighten curly hair. Of course,

Haircoloring is so easy and so widespread now that you can have practically any color you want to try. Few would want to go as far as the rainbow colors of the wig on the right, but all the women below have altered their natural hair color with colorants designed specifically for use at home.

since the advent of the "Afro" hair style, many women have decided to keep their hair as Nature made it, relying on mild shampoos, cream rinses, and a good cut to make it soft and shapely.

Perhaps the most dramatic, delightful, and time-honored way to change your hair is to change its color. Women, and men too, have been experimenting with hair colorants since earliest times. With a little ingenuity, they have turned the most unlikely raw materials into dyes and bleaches. They have used powdered beetles and oak tree roots to dye it black; lemon and elderberry ash to make it blonde; and ground-up henna leaves to turn it flaming red. You could still use natural substances to color your hair—many a bright redhead swears by henna, for example — but

Most women have hair of varying shades. Streaking or highlighting just emphasizes this and gives an allover impression of fairer hair by bleaching individual strands. The process is slow and has to be done properly, but once done, it doesn't need touch-ups as allover color changes do. Strands of hair to be bleached are pulled through a rubber cap that protects the rest of the hair. (Be sure that there are no tears in the cap, or you will have a little circle of bleached hair at the scalp where the bleach has leaked through.) You can see that streaking is not at all easy to do at home, and you'll probably prefer to have it done by expert beauticians at the beauty salon.

for subtlety and sheer ease, you can't beat the products science has provided. Moreover, since hair coloring has become so accepted a part of a woman's prerogative, it's no longer a question of should you or shouldn't you, but do you want to, and if so, which kind?

Both in terms of color and method, you have a wide range of choices before you—everything from bleaching to tinting, streaking, and highlighting. But before you make up your mind, take three things into consideration: your skin tone, your basic hair color, and your way of life. Any new hair color should harmonize, in different ways, with all three. A busy housewife with olive skin and dark brown hair, for example, would be ill-advised to turn herself into a platinum blonde. It would not only look wrong, but would also require more care, in terms of touching up, than she has time for. Her best bet, if she wants to change her look, would be to darken her hair. Raven tresses would bring out the Latin in her.

In fact, for any dark-haired woman to become a blonde requires bleaching, the most drastic form of color change. What happens when you bleach your hair is that you subtract color from it. If you start out with dark hair, it can take a couple of hours to go light, because you have to pass stage by stage from brown, to red, to auburn, to yellow-gold, to pale blonde. It's hard on your hair, and should be done by an expert.

What if your hair is almost, but not quite, blonde already? In that case, your best bet is to use one of the many excellent lighteners

Hair style can help over-
come problems with shape
and features of face. So
take some tips on how to
make the most of yourself.
With a round face, you
can either emphasize the
top part of your head,
or, as here, camouflage
your round cheeks with
hair lying over them. You
will probably find that
short hair is flattering.

Your hair looks best in
a flowing wavy style,
with enough body to widen
your narrow face. Then
let it fall across your
face to cover the jawline.

Your hairstyle aim should
be to add width to your
slender face. Try the
femininity of masses of
curls, or, as here, side
ponytails floating free
in a flurry of soft waves.

ROUND FACE

SQUARE-JAWED

LONG FACE

now on the market. They too, contain a certain amount of the bleaching agent hydrogen peroxide, but in a very mild form. Available in the form of shampoos or rinses, they're easy to use at home, and have a gradual, cumulative effect, lightening and brightening your hair a little bit more with each application.

Another way to highlight your hair—be it dark blonde or light brown—is to have it streaked. It's best to have it done for you, because it's a fairly delicate operation. Streaking involves the selective bleaching of strands of hair, much as the sun bleaches it— and that's the beauty of it. It looks genuinely natural. Moreover, it doesn't require frequent retouching at the roots. Streaking is a fairly lengthy process. The hairdresser works strand by strand, bleaching only a few hairs at a time. To keep the rest of your hair from being bleached as well, she will either put you in a plastic cap, and pull out the strands to be

bleached through little holes in the cap, or wrap the already bleached strands in strips of aluminum foil. It may take a while, but the end result is usually more than worth it.

By far the most popular method of hair coloring is tinting. Quick and efficient, it's a perfect way to add both color and highlights to your hair. If you want to go from gray to brunette, from dark brown to raven, from chestnut to auburn, from pale blonde to gold, tinting is definitely for you.

Tinting colorants fall into three categories: temporary ones, which affect only the outer layer of the hair shaft and wash out after a single shampoo; semipermanent ones, which penetrate a little deeper into the hair shaft and last for several shampoos; and the so-called permanent tints, which completely penetrate the hair shaft and last for numerous shampoos—except, of course, for those tell-tale roots, which will need retouching.

Temporary color changers, which come in

Stay away from heavy bangs —you need to point up the fragile appeal of the rest of your face. Try a fluffy style, with the fullness covering the widest part of your cheeks.

A low forehead becomes no problem at all with bangs that start far back at the crown. With hair over your forehead, no one will ever know if it is low, high, or average.

Emphasize the crown of your head. You are the girl who can look elegant with a soft pile of long hair pinned up in romantic old-world style, or with a short fluffy style high at the crown. But be sure the height is at the top: thickness at the nape of the neck will draw attention straight to the profile line.

HEART-SHAPED FACE

LOW FOREHEAD

PROMINENT NOSE

the form of shampoos and rinses, are helpful if you're in any doubt about whether the new color will suit you. If it doesn't, you can wash it out and try a different shade. If it does, you're all set to proceed with a more permanent tint in the same shade. If you've taken the leap, and used a permanent tint, but you don't like the results, go to your hairdresser. She can correct the color. But you can avoid this kind of hassle altogether by testing the tint on a snip of your hair. There's no better way to see how it will take.

Another thing you must do before using any colorant is to test its reaction on your skin. (What's the good of a divine new hair color if your scalp hurts?) Simply put a little of the tint on the inside of your elbow, and don't wash it off for 24 hours. If no irritation develops, it's safe to use the tint. If there are signs of redness, however, you'd better throw away the bottle and try another brand.

A final tip about tinting: don't do it just

before giving yourself a permanent. Although permanent wave lotions don't affect natural hair color, they can lift some of the color from newly tinted hair. Your best bet is to color your hair about ten days after a permanent.

Last but not least, what about cutting and styling your hair? Both usually mean a trip to the beauty salon—and it's absolutely essential to find a good one. The hairdresser must be someone you can trust, not only with your confidences, but also with your hair. Does he take pains to get your cut exactly right? Does he give you a style that's easy to keep and simple to alter—quickly and flatteringly— for special occasions? If he does, count your blessings—you're a lucky woman.

It can help a lot if you yourself know what suits you. Many factors are involved: your height and weight, the length of your neck and breadth of your forehead, the shape of your nose, ears, and chin—even your glasses, if you wear them all the time. Have a glance

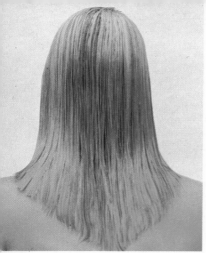

Above: this cut for long hair is slightly layered at the back to give shape to the head. The point is centered exactly on the shoulderblades, and the ends are cut obliquely.

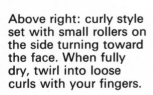

Above right: curly style set with small rollers on the side turning toward the face. When fully dry, twirl into loose curls with your fingers.

Above left: middle part, with hair held behind ears with small combs.

Left: bangs pulled back from the forehead are held by barrettes. Hair is parted in the middle.

at the illustrations on the previous pages. They may give you some new ideas.

As always, though, the secret lies in finding what's right for *you*. Don't let yourself get hung up—either on the dictates of current fashion, or on what's supposed to be right for your age, your face, or your figure. Mystifyingly, even the wrongest hair style can be perfect on a woman, simply because it flatters her own particular looks. Experiment a little, and above all, care for your hair. Long or short, plain or fancy, lustrously healthy hair is worth its weight in gold—or silver, or chestnut, or raven, or auburn, or ...

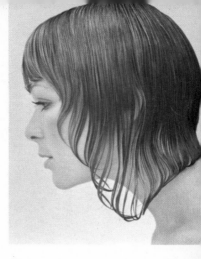

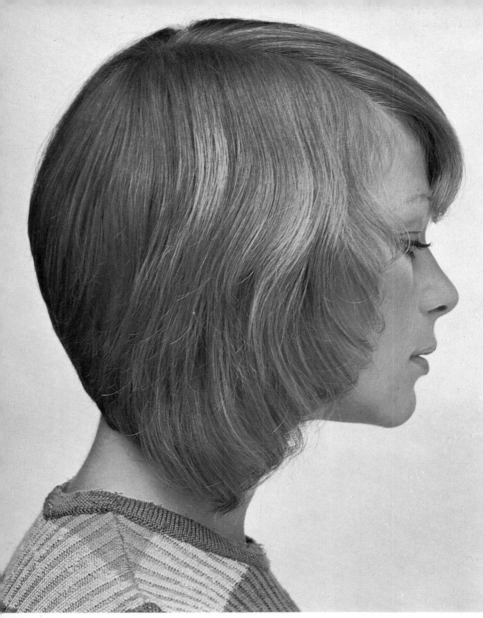

Above: this style is semi-blunt, layered at the back, very short. At the sides the hair is artfully cut short at the front and longer over the ears.
Left: simply blown dry.

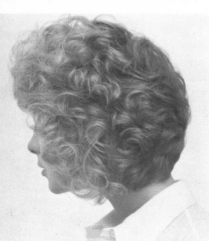

Left: again set in small locks by the curler, and held by clips until cool, this style is "arranged" by a brisk head-shaking. Wispy curls are then formed with the fingers.

Far left: a curly head set lock by lock with an electric curler and held with clips until the hair has completely cooled. The short hair at the neck is waved gently toward the front.

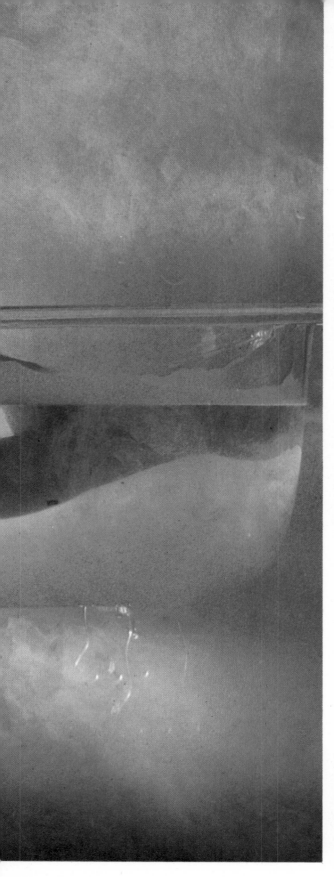

The Bath: Treat and Treatment

5

Taking a bath or shower has become such a habit that most of us don't give it much thought. Nor, alas, do we often give it much time. In fact, many a woman, her mind racing ahead over all the things she's got to do during the day, tends to bathe like an efficiency expert. Having snatched a free five minutes, she hops into the tub or shower, soaps up, rinses off, and hops out again, clean as a whistle in the twinkling of an eye.

Of course, there's a lot to be said for this method. It's fast, it's efficient, and it leaves you feeling fresh and invigorated. But we all need to unwind from time to time, and there's nothing like a good old-fashioned bath—long and relaxing—to take out the kinks and restore your tranquility. We all know what a luxury it is to have a few moments all to ourselves, and many of us

A beauty bath can be a delightful spell of self-indulgence, with all the cares of your world on the other side of the locked bathroom door. Plan a long luxurious soak—you can even enjoy a bit of reading.

Shaving is easier if you use soap or foam with a safety razor, and make sure that your skin is absolutely dry before using an electric razor.

Chemical depilatories are efficient and leave your skin free of hair for several weeks. However, do make a 24-hour test before using a new one.

have come to regard the bath as a real haven of rest. Just reclining in a tubful of warm water, and letting your thoughts drift, can do wonders for both body and soul.

But bathing can mean more than enjoying some peace and quiet while you cleanse and refresh yourself. It can also offer a delightful opportunity to pamper yourself, to tone and nourish your skin from head to toe, and to attend to all the little details that affect the way you look and feel. Simply take advantage of it, and the humble bath can become a heavenly beauty treatment.

Ideally, every woman should treat herself to a beauty bath every day, but if you find that you simply can't fit it in on a daily basis, make it a twice or thrice, weekly treat. Any way you do it, you'll find yourself relishing the times when the bathroom becomes your

own private beauty clinic.

To make the bathroom a place in which you can really feel pampered, lavish a little care and attention on it. It's always easier to relax in attractive and comfortable surroundings. Try, too, to make it as much your own room as possible while you're using it. If, for example, you have small children who leave toys and rubber ducks around, stash them away in a box or cupboard before you take your bath. It seems a small thing, but it contributes greatly to the feeling of peace that's so essential to a truly relaxing session in the tub.

If you feel the slightest hesitation about really pampering yourself with a beauty bath, remember that women the world over have been discovering its delights and reaping its benefits since time immemorial. After all, you're not being half as extravagant as Nero's wife Poppaea, who used to bathe in gallons of fresh milk, or as Mary, Queen of Scots, whose idea of the bath beautiful was a tubful of fine wine.

Now, what kind of a bath are you going to treat yourself to? One that is neither too hot nor too cold is the most relaxing, and it's good for all skin types. When it comes to the bath essence you choose, your skin type becomes a decisive factor.

Foams and bubble baths usually contain detergents, which tend to wash away natural oils. So if you have dry skin, and you like the luxurious feeling of bathing in a sea of foam, be sure to choose a brand that contains a water-soluble oil. Incidentally, the new water-soluble bath oils are a real boon. They not only leave the skin feeling smooth and supple, but also make the tub easy to clean.

Alternatively, you dry-skin types may want to try a more exotic bath essence. Two tablespoons of almond, avocado, or sesame oil in the water—with a drop or two of perfume for added fragrance—makes a marvelously soothing and nourishing conditioner for dry skin.

If you have oily skin and you want to try something new and different in the way of a bath essence, squeeze a lemon or two into the bath water. It smells beautiful and leaves your skin feeling wonderfully fresh and clean. Another ingenious recipe for oily skin is the addition to your bath of a few small portions of oatmeal tied up in cheese-cloth. It turns the water milky, and absorbs oil well.

Special ingredients added, it's time to step into the tub and soak up the goodness—and you should soak your whole body, except for your hands and bosom, where the skin is especially delicate, for about 20 minutes before washing. A headrest at the end of the tub makes it easier to lean back, close your eyes, and forget your cares.

When you begin washing, use as little soap as possible, especially if you have dry skin. Most foams and bath oils make the use of soap unnecessary. Even without them, water alone is sufficient for cleansing all but three special areas: the underarms, feet, and genital region. Where the latter is concerned, washing should be the merest mini-shampoo, limited strictly to the pubic hair. Water is all that Nature meant to have used for washing inside the vagina. Soap strips away the delicate oils that keep it lubricated.

Before stepping out of the tub, splash yourself all over with cool water. It's a great way to tone the skin and close the pores, particularly if your skin tends to be a bit oily. Then towel yourself dry, alternately patting and rubbing. Pay special attention to the skin on your upper arms, which, as you get older, has a tendency to develop a slightly rough, goose pimply look from decreased circulatory activity.

Another area that may call for special care is your thighs and bottom on which, again as you get older, you may begin to notice the slightly dimpled effect that is sometimes called "cellulite." The best way to tackle this problem is to coat the dimpled area with baby oil after your bath, and then massage it in—kneading, wringing, and pummeling

Waxing is a very old way of removing hair—but it is still an efficient one. Greater satisfaction is assured, however, if it is done by an expert.

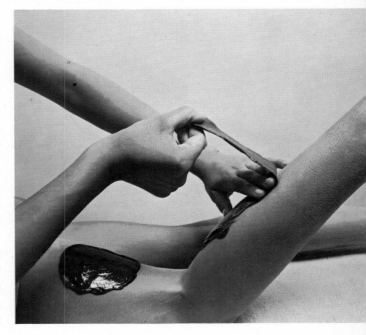

gently but firmly. The idea is to stimulate the circulation for, like goose flesh, dimpling is caused by decreased circulatory activity. Exercise can help too, of course, but exercise chiefly benefits the muscles, and dimpling is a problem that affects the upper tissues only.

If you have very dry skin, you might wish to coat your whole body with baby oil, or a fragrant body lotion, massaging it in with gentle, circular movements. Whatever your skin type, though, you will probably want to oil the rough skin on your elbows, heels, and soles of your feet. This should be done after rubbing off the hard or flaky outer layer of skin with a pumice stone.

Just after your bath is the best time to remove superfluous body hair, because it's been softened up by the water. There's a wide range of methods to choose from, the most common being simple shaving, with either an electric or plain safety razor. If you use a safety razor, first coat your legs or underarms with soap or foam to help the blade glide smoothly over the skin. When you're finished, rinse the shaven areas well and, if you have any nicks, close them up with styptic pencil.

Does shaving cause hair to grow in faster or thicker? No. If it did, why wouldn't balding men be shaving their heads like crazy? The fact is that shaven hair, on legs or underarms, has been chopped off "square-headed," and thus tends to look and feel a bit more stubbly when it grows back.

Abrasive mitts, designed for use on legs only, work on much the same principle as a razor, except that they wear down the hair rather than cut it off. In fact, they act like the finest of fine sandpapers, gently rubbing away superfluous hair without damaging the skin beneath it.

Waxing is another often-used method of defuzzing. Quick and efficient, it works well on all smooth surfaces, including the upper lip. Any wax depilatory must be heated slightly before being applied to the skin. It is spread over the surface in a thin strip, left to cool, and then peeled off. The hair, which has become embedded in the wax while it was warm, is pulled out with it, leaving the skin satiny smooth. Waxing's disadvantage is that it's a bit painful—rather like tearing a strip of adhesive away from the skin. It's best to have it done by an expert, who will do the whole thing so quickly you'll hardly have time to say "ouch."

Chemical depilatories, like waxing, work well on either large or small surfaces, but preferably not on underarms if your skin is sensitive. They come in the form of liquids, creams, pastes, and foams, and work by softening up the protein that gives hair its strength. Because the protein in skin and hair is very similar, any chemical depilatory should be used with extreme care. Be sure to test it first on a small unnoticeable patch of skin. Wait 24 hours, and then, if the area shows no sign of irritation, you're free to proceed. Leave it on only as long as the instructions stipulate, usually five to ten minutes. Then, simply wipe the area with a cloth, rinse well, and presto! the hair is gone. Like waxing, chemical depilatories are quick and efficient, and leave the skin free of hair for several weeks.

For most of us, it's almost second nature to apply a deodorant, antiperspirant, or combination of the two practically as soon as we step out of the tub. But if you've just shaved under your arms, it's wise to wait 24 hours first. Newly shaven skin—especially if it's been nicked—is particularly sensitive, and can become irritated through contact with any chemical.

Deodorants and antiperspirants, by the way, are not the same thing, though the two terms are often used as if they were. Deodorants work by reducing the bacteria normally found on the skin, so that any perspiration has less raw material to work on. Antiperspirants actually reduce perspiration by suppressing the action of the sweat glands, though not entirely; to accomplish that, they'd also have to affect the nerve cells, which could be dangerous.

In the long run, a combination deodorant and antiperspirant, preferably one of the scentless varieties, is your best bet. If you're

Above: a cream depilatory may help to avoid those nasty nicks from a razor, but be sure you pick one designed for delicate skin. Right: spray deodorants have become much more popular for their ease of use, but do take care not to breathe in the spray. Below: a roll-on deodorant is another easy way to avoid perspiration smell.

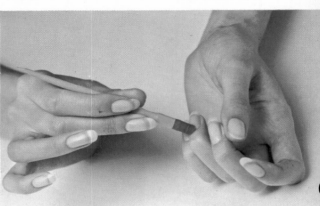

like most of us, however, you'll find that you gradually become immune to the chemicals in any one product—be it spray, roll-on, lotion, or cream. So it's wise to switch brands from time to time.

While we're on the subject of body fresheners, what about vaginal deodorants, mouthwashes, and foot sprays? Though it may seem odd at first glance to lump them all together, the fact is that they all work on basically the same principle. Each is especially designed to reduce the bacteria which, in combination with natural body moistures, cause odor. None of them, if used properly, can do you the slightest harm. Nor, by the same token, are their beneficial effects, though perfectly genuine, very long lasting.

In that case, are they really necessary? Well, strictly speaking, no. If you take baths and brush your teeth regularly, you will be as clean and sweet-smelling as anyone could wish. But unquestionably, fresheners can have an added, intangible value in terms of their psychological effects on you. The sparkly fresh taste of a mouthwash, the menthol-cool feeling of a foot spray, the

sheer knowledge of having used a vaginal deodorant may give you extra confidence in yourself. And if extra self-confidence is all you need to bring out the swan in you, use as many fresheners as you like!

Just after your bath is a good time to attend to your hands and feet. Both nails and cuticles have been softened up, and are easier to work on. If your toenails need cutting, now's the time to do it, using a nail clip and cutting straight across the width of the nail (the square corners prevent ingrown nails). Remember to leave enough nail to cover the sensitive tips of your toes.

Now, on both hands and feet, gently push back the cuticle at the base of each nail with an orange stick. You can also deftly snip away any little hangnails. If, however, you find that the whole cuticle on any nail is particularly rough and thick, do not—repeat, do not—be tempted to cut it away with your clippers. This will only make it grow back tougher. Instead, soften it up with a cuticle cream, but don't leave it on too long; cuticle creams can also soften the nail.

3

4

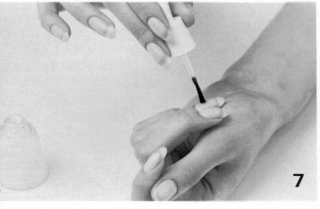

7

8

Giving yourself a manicure at home isn't difficult.
1. Carefully remove the old polish with cotton moistened with remover, and wipe thoroughly clean.
2. Shape your nails gently with an emery board. being careful to use it in only one direction.
3. Relax and soak your fingernails for a few minutes in warm soapy water, to soften cuticles.
4. Take a towel and dry each nail individually.
5. Wrap a piece of absorbent cotton around an orange stick, dip in cuticle remover, and press gently around the cuticle and under the nail.
6. Wait a minute, then push the cuticles gently back with the soft tip of the orange stick.
7. Start your nail polish with a protective under-coat of clear polish, and allow to dry completely.
8. Finish with a coat of colored polish. Start with one central stroke, and then fill in sides.

If, in, fact, you have trouble with soft or brittle nails, you might try gelatin tablets or powder, taken two or three times a day, to build up their strength. In the meantime, if you have a broken nail, you don't have to pare it down. You can patch it. Simply smooth a piece of tissue over both sides of the nail at the torn point, then fix it with a coat of clear nail polish or special nail-mending cement.

To protect your nails—and even more important, your hands—be sure to wear rubber gloves whenever you wash the dishes

79

or handle household chemicals. Frequent exposure to soaps and detergents, bleaches and polishes, can age the delicate skin on your hands amazingly fast. In fact, badly treated hands can look years older than the face they belong to. Use a hand cream or lotion often to keep your hands soft and smooth. Also, guard them against the sun— it not only dries out the skin, but it also encourages the appearance of those little brown marks, sometimes called "liver spots," we're all prone to as we get older.

Sometimes a woman will neglect her hands because she has a tendency to bite her nails. Yet she is just the person who will benefit most from regular hand care and manicuring. The more attention she lavishes on both hands and nails, the less inclined she will feel to undo the good work. This cure through care works well, as many an ex-nail biter will tell you.

If you are already looking after your hands properly, you're no doubt also an adept at giving yourself a manicure, and know that beautiful nails are the result of continual care. This doesn't mean, of course, that you have to work at them every day, but it does mean that they should be filed and buffed regularly to give them shape and finish. Try to use an emery board when you file your nails, and shape them when they are at their hardest—in other words, not directly after your bath. Buffing can be done anytime, and works best if you use a buffing cream first.

Clear or colored nail polish can do a lot to enhance the appearance of your nails. Before you apply it, make sure that the nail surface is clean. Remove any traces of a previous coat with nail polish remover, wash, and let dry. Then apply as many coats of polish as you wish, letting each dry thoroughly before applying the next. Every coat should be as thin as possible, and applied with quick, definite strokes. Some polishes

Some women use one scent that becomes identified with them. Others choose a different perfume for a different mood or time. Either way, a woman who moves in a subtle drift of fragrance is a delight to everyone around her.

adhere better if a prime coat is used first. If you want to increase the durability of the polish, a special kind of top coat is also available.

The last steps in your head-to-toe beauty session are in many ways the most fun, because they add the "pretty-perfect" finish you want the world to ·notice. Cleansed, relaxed, and refreshed, you make up your face, fix your hair, and spray or smooth on that final, indispensable luxury, fragrance.

Whether it be a real perfume or one of its subtler cousins—cologne or toilet water—scent weaves a gossamer web of glamour and femininity around you. Used artfully—at the base of the throat and behind the ears, on temples, inner wrists, and elbows, and perhaps, too, at the back of your knees—it can be a silent, but delicately persuasive spokesman for the special person you are.

Select your perfume with the utmost care, testing its interaction with your own unique chemistry by dabbing it on the inside of your wrist or elbow before buying it. Don't make up your mind too quickly. Perfume should be left on a pulse spot for 20 minutes or so to give it time to be activated by the warmth of your body.

It's lovely to have several scents on hand. The more you have, the more creative you can be in matching your fragrance to your mood, or the time of day. There's a whole wide range of subtly different scents to choose from. Some speak of cool, misty forests, others of sunlit fields of flowers. Some carry the freshness of a sea breeze, others the sweet tang of fruits and spices. Some are brightly sophisticated, others warmly sensual.

The choice, of course, is up to you, and, in the last analysis, mere words fail utterly to convey the true, evocative quality of any perfume. But that's just the point, isn't it? Perfume, like the sparkle in your eyes, takes up where words leave off.

The Magic Word "Diet"

6

Open almost any magazine these days and you'll find yourself reading about some incredible new diet. Doctors and nutritionists, beauty experts and health food enthusiasts—they're all in there pitching, telling us just why and how we should lose weight. The range of "wonder diets" is phenomenal—and so are the claims made for them. Try this, try that, and those extra pounds will vanish in no time, leaving us fit, sleek, and slender as willow wands.

Not surprisingly, foreigners often get the impression that dieting is one of our national pastimes. Indeed, it would be hard to find a single red-blooded American, male or female, who is not either on a diet, just off a diet, or about to start a diet. Are we getting obsessional about it? Well, yes, perhaps so, but there's method in our madness. As a nation, we're affluent and knowledgeable. We like to eat, but we know that it's wise to be slim. We're surrounded by delicious foods in plenty, but we're aware that good health and good looks don't go hand in hand with overeating.

So what do we do? We overindulge ourselves, then suffer the tortures of the damned with harsh self-disciplinary measures. The only trouble is, our indulgence is always one step ahead of our self-discipline. The result? We manage to be pound wise and pound foolish at one and the same time. Despite our national passion for dieting, some 30 per cent of us under 45 are overweight and, it seems, getting more so every year. Between 45 and 55, the figure soars—or should we say expands—to include over 50 per cent of the men and 75 per cent of the women.

How did so many of us get into the overweight category? Certainly not through glandular trouble or fluid retention, which are fairly serious ailments, affecting only a tiny fraction of the population. So how then? The reasons are as varied as human nature. Some of us just got into the habit of eating too much when we were kids. Others of us acquired the habit later on, eating away to reward or console ourselves, allay anxiety or relieve boredom, finish up the leftovers, or make up for the cigarettes we have given up.

Paradoxically, some people eat most when they are most concerned about the way they look or feel. Not so paradoxically, a few overeat to beef up their self-image, unconsciously associating physical size with ego strength. For some, fattening foods have a special attraction just because they are forbidden fruit. For many others, big meals have simply become a way of life.

The motives vary, but the outcome is the same—and so is the state of mind that develops as we put on weight. With mingled hope and despair, we fling ourselves into some new crash diet, give it up, put on a few more pounds, and try another madcap slimming technique. What's wrong with these desperate remedies? In a word, a lot.

To start with, there are the numerous diet foods, liquids, crackers, and cookies, designed to be taken before, or instead of, meals. Their purpose is to swell up inside you, curbing your appetite by making you feel full. They can be a great help—provided they *do* curb your appetite—and many people

Keep a regular weekly appointment with your scales (those daily fluctuations are usually insignificant)—and eat to keep your weight just where you want it.

swear by them. Others find them unsatisfying in taste, and disillusioning as far as calories go. For they do contain calories, and continual munching on diet foods can actually put on weight.

Then there are those evil little items, diet pills. True, they curb your appetite, but only while you're on them. They also make you nervous and jumpy, and are genuinely addictive—and who needs that?

Crash diets are a dime a dozen, and go in and out of fashion like pop stars. A few of them are exotic, requiring large amounts of special foods like peanuts and oranges, honey and wheat germ, caviar and nectarines. Fun for a day or two, but after that, a plain bore. A little less tedious and more sensible is the famous grapefruit diet. This one works on the principle that half a grapefruit, or a glass of unsweetened grapefruit juice before each meal, will act as kindling, helping to burn up the calories in the other food you're about to consume. But even grapefruit begins to pall after a while, as many people have found.

When it comes right down to it, the only crash diet that makes any kind of sense is that old standby, the low-carbohydrate diet. You know the routine: a drastic reduction of all those calorie-laden starches and sugars— such as bread, potatoes, pasta, candy, cookies, and cakes. (The high-fat and high-protein diets work on the same basic principle. Though they allow you to step up your intake of high-energy foods like lean meat or oils, they also require you to cut down on carbohydrates.)

A completely carbohydrate-free diet produces much the same effects as that far more dubious slimming technique, outright fasting.

These effects are loss of weight, and loss of appetite, but also loss of energy. It's great for losing a few pounds fast—if you don't mind feeling a bit weary as well—but it's hard on your system, and should never be undertaken without your doctor's approval. In fact, the only low-carbohydrate diet most doctors agree with calls for the daily consumption of about 100 grams of carbohydrates—taken, of course, from natural sources such as fresh fruits and vegetables.

By far the most successful weight losing program to date is the one created by the Weight Watchers, and emulated by other slimming clubs. Whatever specific diet they advocate is firmly bolstered by the psychology they employ. You get group support for your efforts, group criticism for your failures, and group praise for your achievements. You keep tabs on your fellow dieters, they keep tabs on you—and for long enough to change not only your weight, but your appestat. In case you don't already know what that is, it's the physically nonexistent, but emotionally real, corner of your brain that determines your appetite. It's the conning tower that cons you into eating more than you need, and the elusive something that crash diets can't touch.

All quickie diets have the severe drawback of being temporary measures. Nobody sticks with them for very long, and even if they helped you lose a few pounds, they wouldn't have changed a thing except your weight. But that's what it's all about, you say. No it isn't, as any ex-crash dieter will tell you. Your real target is your appestat, your eating habits, your whole attitude toward food. Pounds lost in a crash diet return

84

The Right Weight for You

Height ft. ins.	Small frame	Medium frame	Large frame
4 8	87–93	91–102	99–114
4 9	89–96	93–105	101–117
4 10	91–99	96–108	104–120
4 11	95–102	99–111	107–123
5 0	97–105	102–114	110–126
5 1	100–108	105–117	113–129
5 2	103–111	108–121	116–133
5 3	106–114	111–125	120–137
5 4	109–118	115–130	124–141
5 5	113–122	119–135	128–145
5 6	117–126	123–138	132–149
5 7	121–130	127–142	136–153
5 8	125–135	131–146	140–158
5 9	129–139	135–150	145–163
5 10	133–143	139–155	148–169

© Dr Anthony Barnard Harris

Overweight usually results from a pattern of eating, so husband and wife often both get too heavy. This couple (wife shown left before going on a diet) lost 42 lbs. between them on a low carbohydrate diet, and by working at it together, are changing their food habits to a "thinking thin" routine.

as soon as you stop playing your little game. To succeed permanently—and anyone can— you've got to change your whole outlook on food and eating.

Slimming clubs are past masters at helping people accomplish this aim. You can easily do it yourself, though, provided you're farseeing enough to think in terms of permanent changes in, rather than brief aberrations from, your normal approach to food.

The first thing to do is equip yourself with some facts. Do you know approximately what weight is right for your frame? If not, a quick glance at the chart above will tell you. Do you know how many calories you burn up during the day? The answer, for the moderately active woman of average height and build, is approximately 2,000. Naturally, a fairly short, small-boned woman needs, and burns up, somewhat fewer calories per day, while a tall woman with a more generous frame needs and burns up slightly more. But the principle is the same for all. Take in a few less calories than you burn up, and your body will make up the balance from its reserves of fat. Take in a few more, and your body will add to those reserves. Note this, too: every 3500 calories above what you use up will make an extra pound. It would be rather hard to consume 3500 extra calories in a single day, or even during a weekend, but over the course of a week or two . . . !

Naturally, the harder you work, the more calories you burn up. The U.S. Department of Agriculture has come up with a nifty little guide to calorie usage per hour, per activity. We've included a brief summary of it to give you some idea of the fluctuations in calorie burning that most of us experience.

Calorie Expenditure

Type of Activity	Calories Per Hour
SEDENTARY ACTIVITIES, such as reading; writing; eating; watching television or movies; listening to the radio; sewing; playing cards; and typing, miscellaneous office work, and other activities done while sitting that require little or no arm movement.	80–100
LIGHT ACTIVITIES, such as preparing and cooking food; doing dishes; dusting; handwashing small articles of clothing; ironing; walking slowly; personal care; miscellaneous office work and other activities done while standing that require some arm movement; and rapid typing and other activities done while sitting that are more strenuous.	110–160
MODERATE ACTIVITIES, such as making beds; mopping and scrubbing; sweeping; light polishing and waxing; laundering by machine; light gardening and carpentry work; walking moderately fast; other activities done while standing that require moderate arm movement; and activities done while sitting that require more vigorous arm movement.	170–240
VIGOROUS ACTIVITIES, such as heavy scrubbing and waxing; hand washing large articles of clothing; hanging out clothes; stripping beds; other heavy work; walking fast; bowling; golfing; and gardening.	250–350
STRENUOUS ACTIVITIES, such as swimming; playing tennis; running; bicycling; dancing; skiing; and playing football.	350 and more

You'll notice that the biggest calorie burners are strenuous things like sports and exercise. So what about these activities as a way of losing weight? By themselves, neither will cure a weight problem. But allied to dieting, they can do wonders to tone and firm up your figure.

So on to the nitty-gritty: food. If you're going to establish a good relationship with it, one that will result in a healthier, slimmer you for the rest of your life, you'll want to bear five simple rules in mind: shop thin, cook thin, drink thin, eat thin, and think thin. They come straight from Eileen Ford, the woman who founded one of the most successful model agencies in the world, and they have the backing of doctors and nutritionists alike.

First, shop thin. This simply means that you buy the leanest cuts of meat, the freshest fish, poultry, fruits and vegetables. Make these your chief concern when you go to the supermarket, and skip those calorie-filled, unnutritious, and expensive goodies, such as brownies and coffee cake, cracker snacks and pizza pie, soft drinks and ice cream. If you don't have them around, you won't be tempted to indulge in them.

Second, cook thin. This is where imagination, a good cookbook, and a calorie counter combine to produce marvelous meals that don't add pounds. Experiment with herbs and spices. Learn to dress up lean cuts of meat, grilled fish, and broiled poultry in such a way that they become the high point of the meal, rather than a mere filler before a rich dessert. There are some excellent meat, fish, and poultry cookbooks on the market,

Anything you do burns calories—whether it is nonstrenuous sewing or energetic tennis playing. Check the chart opposite to find out how many calories your ordinary activities use up. It can give you an idea of how much food you need.

U.S. Department of Agriculture chart summary reprinted here by courtesy of Trident Press, New York, from *Eileen Ford's Book of Model Beauty.*

as well as some superb vegetable and salad cookbooks. You'll be surprised at the many ways of cooking such basics as carrots, beans, and leafy greens. If you feel incomplete without something sweet for dessert, inaugurate the habit of serving fresh fruit, such as cantaloupe or apricots, grapes or berries, at the end of a meal. A gourmet dinner doesn't leave you feeling heavy afterward—but rich chocolate cake or blueberry pie will.

Third, drink thin. Stick to dietary soft drinks, coffee and tea without sugar, skimmed milk, and wines in preference to beer and hard liquor. If you can, also avoid drinking with meals. Liquids taken between meals seem to be less fattening.

Fourth, eat thin. This means eating only at meal times. If you must snack, have only things like raw carrots and celery, tomatoes

or a diet drink. It also means eating small portions, and slowly, as though each bite were a rare treat. Think about and enjoy the food as you eat it. If you wolf it down, you'll find yourself looking forward hungrily to the next meal.

Finally, think thin. There are three tricks to following this rule. First, literally brainwash yourself out of certain foods. Don't think of gooey desserts, candy bars, french fries, rich sauces, mashed potatoes, and heaps of pasta as "forbidden fruit." Think of them instead as unhealthy, ugly-making glop, utterly beneath your notice—and pity the poor fools who find them interesting.

Second, make "balance" your watchword, not only during the day—we all know about the required daily quotas of nutriments— but from day to day as well. Suppose, for example, that it's Christmas or Thanksgiving, that a big lunch at a friend's falls on the same day as a sumptuous dinner out with your husband, or that you find yourself going into a skid and slipping back into your old eating habits for a day or two. Just regard it as a temporary aberration from the norm, and balance it up with a couple of days of careful cutting back. Don't, by any means, take it as the signal for defeat, declare yourself a total failure, and fling yourself into an orgy of overeating. You are, after all, only human, and you don't have to punish yourself for a brief fall from grace by throwing away all the good you've already done yourself. The test of a good dieter is that she, or he, can continue on his merry, healthful way despite a few slip-ups.

The third trick in thinking thin is to regard food in terms of its cosmetic values. Obviously, genuine vitality, lustrous hair, bright eyes, and clear skin are an asset to any woman. They all go hand in hand with a good diet. Choose your food carefully, and it can be a strong ally in the beauty game.

Have a look at the "beauty foods" listed below. For a change, they're not lumped into the old home economics categories of proteins, vitamins, minerals, fats, and carbohydrates. Instead, they're arranged purely

When you look at the lavish displays of food at the supermarket, think of it as ingredients for beauty and health—and pick the ones you need.

Foods for Health and Beauty

Vitality, Stamina, and Calm Nerves	Lean meat (especially liver and kidney); fish, poultry, and dairy products; brewers yeast, whole grains, wheat germ, and soybeans; fruits, fruit juices, nuts, raisins, honey, molasses, iodized salt, spinach, fish and vegetable oils.
Clear Skin, Shiny Hair, Strong Nails	Fish, liver, dairy products; whole grains, and gelatin; leafy green vegetables, green peppers, tomatoes, carrots, and avocados; citrus fruits, apples, apricots, melons, and cantaloupe; nuts, fish and vegetable oils.
Bright Eyes	Dairy products; liver and kidney; fish, nuts, and whole grains; carrots, apricots, berries, cantaloupe; and leafy green vegetables.
Healthy Teeth and Gums	Milk fortified with Vitamin D, cheese, eggs, cream, and yoghurt; citrus fruits, tomatoes, green peppers, apples, berries, tuna, salmon, herring, sardines; broccoli, turnip greens, almonds, and molasses.

and simply according to their effect on the way you look and feel.

Finally, how about a word for those of us who are already thin, and worried about it? You may be the envy of many another woman, but that doesn't help much if you feel distressed by your lack of curves.

The first thing to do is to check out your problem with a doctor, to make sure there's no medical reason for your excessive slenderness. If there is not, your plan of action must be the exact opposite of your too curvaceous sister: increase your calorie intake and decrease your level of activity. Eileen Ford suggests having a 300-calorie drink three times a day. (See your calorie counter for the most supergumsluptious drinks around).

This will add at least 900 calories to your daily intake; but be sure to have these instant fatteners sufficiently long before your meals to ensure that you don't ruin your appetite. Another thing you can do is drink a glass of wine before dinner—it's a traditional appetite whetter. Finally, make sure you're getting enough rest. A too active body has a hard time gaining weight.

Whether already slim, or on the way to being slim, every woman's chief aim must be good health. So watch what you eat. Food is not only the fuel of life, but the stuff of which natural good looks are made.

Try munching crisp celery as a between-meal snack, You'll find it to be a tasty treat, low in calories.

Exercise can help you reshape your familiar old self closer to the dream image you have. If that means you want to fatten up your calves, thin down your thighs, firm up your bustline, or reduce your waist, all you need do is pick out the exercise described for your problem in the following pages —and do that exercise with unfailing regularity.

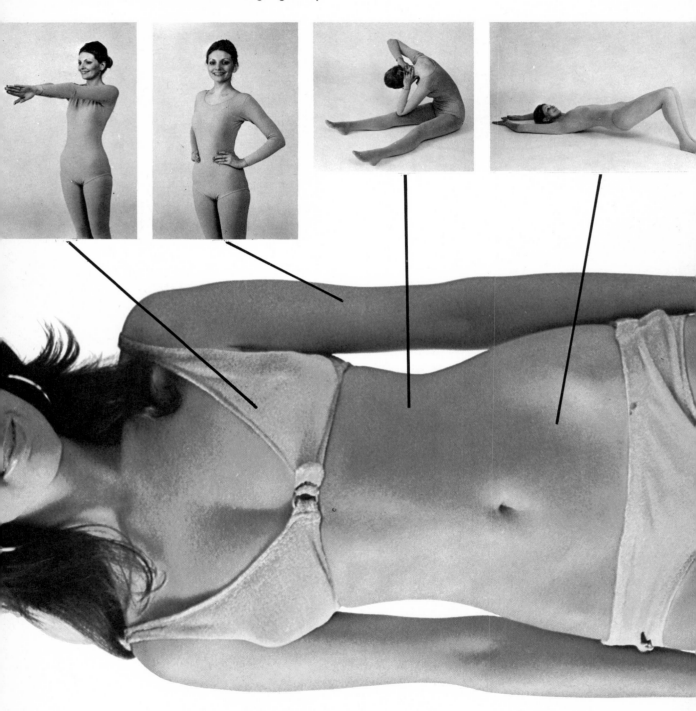

Be Firm With Your Figure

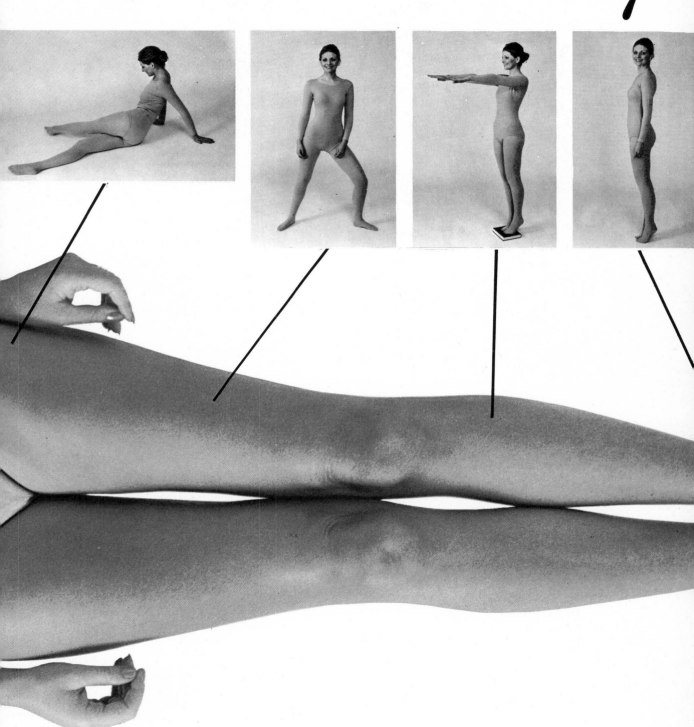

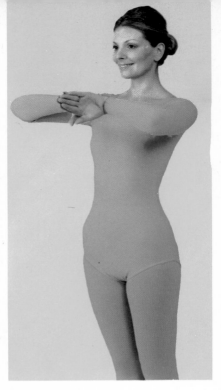

Bustline

Improve your bustline with a breaststroke on dry land. Stand erect with your arms at your sides. Draw arms to shoulder level with elbows bent, hands together, palms out. Stretch arms forward, keeping palms out. Move your arms to the sides as if you were swimming. Drop elbows, bring hands together in front. again at shoulder height, and repeat this several times.

Whatever your age, weight, or lifestyle, there's one thing you must give yourself if you value the woman you are. It's at one and the same time a tonic, a life preserver, and an essential prerequisite for a beautiful and well-cared-for body. What is this miraculous panacea? In a nutshell, it's simply exercise.

By itself, exercise cannot alter your weight, but it can dramatically alter your figure, reshaping your curves in all the right ways. Remember, many a man likes "a lot of woman," provided her curves are under control. It can trim inches from upper arms and midriff, waistline and hips, thighs and bottom, not to mention strengthening the vital muscles around the breasts.

By toning and tightening the body's outer layer of muscles, exercise can help restore the delightful allover firmness of youth, and, if begun early enough, can make the vicelike grip of girdles and foundation garments unnecessary. Bear this in mind if you've been

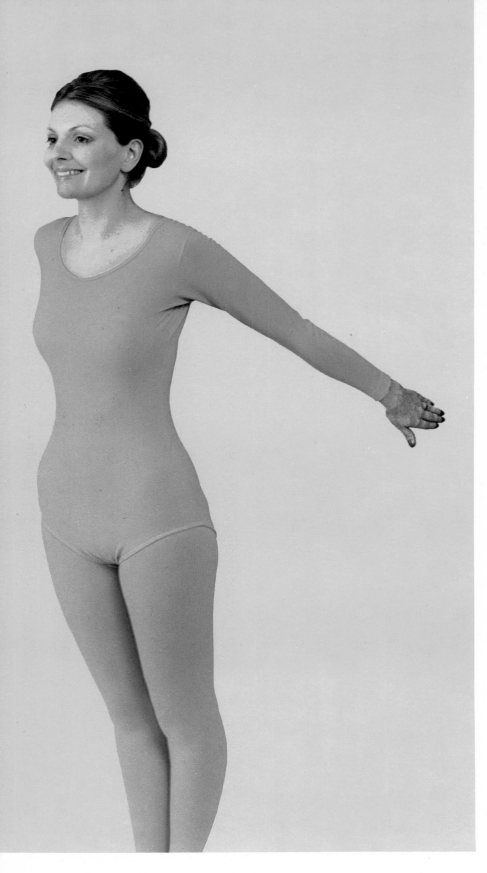

Another breast improver is to place your right fist in your left palm and push with the left arm to the right, while resisting with the right arm. If you're doing it properly, you'll feel your breast lifting. Then try it with the right arm pushing the left.

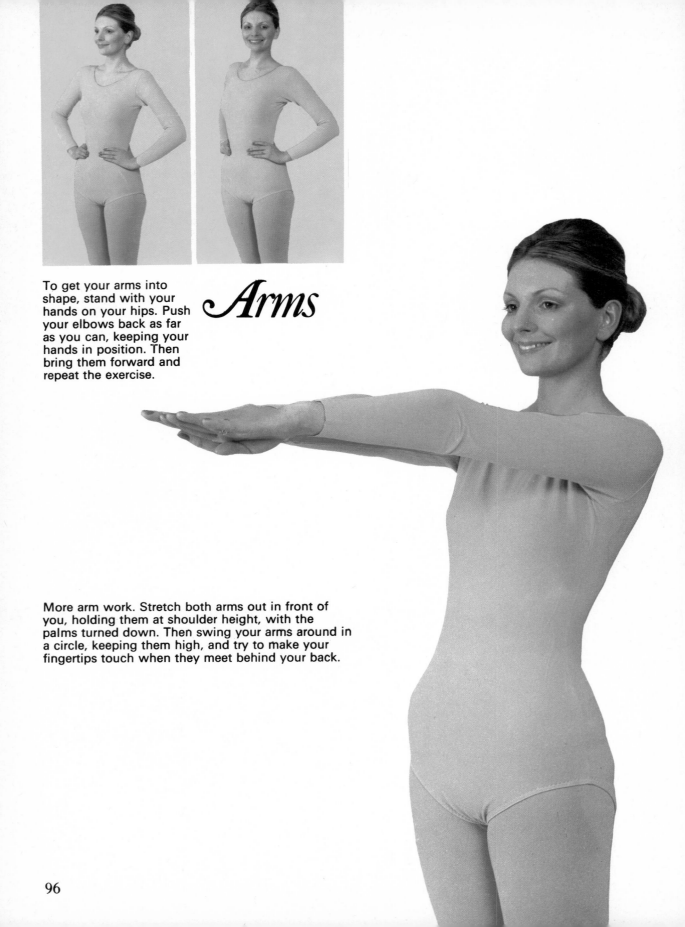

To get your arms into shape, stand with your hands on your hips. Push your elbows back as far as you can, keeping your hands in position. Then bring them forward and repeat the exercise.

Arms

More arm work. Stretch both arms out in front of you, holding them at shoulder height, with the palms turned down. Then swing your arms around in a circle, keeping them high, and try to make your fingertips touch when they meet behind your back.

congratulating yourself on how slender you already are; it's just as easy to be skinny and flabby as it is to be fat and flabby.

Exercise, by improving the action of your heart, lungs, and body chemistry, can increase your stamina, give you a new lease on life, and even increase your longevity. This is just as true whichever side of 50 you're on; energy makes energy, and the more active you are, the more active you will remain.

Through releasing muscular tension—and we are all prone to that—exercise can increase your serenity and ability to cope with things. It's a proven fact that a few well-chosen exercises at the end of a trying day can refresh and restore you more effectively than any cocktail or tranquilizer yet invented. Best of all, regular exercising can endow you with those two characteristic attributes of lovely women everywhere: grace and vitality.

With all these good things going for it, you might think we'd all be exercising like mad. But we're not. Why? Because exercise

has always seemed too boring, too time-consuming, or just plain too much hard work. How can anything this good for you be anything but hard work? Easily; but we'll get to that in a minute. Just for now, let's examine how you in particular react to the word "exercise". Your instinctive response is the best indication of just how much of this precious commodity you're allowing yourself these days.

If, for example, you're one of the 25 million women already reaping the benefits of regular exercise, the mere mention of the word probably makes you glow with pride and pleasure. If, however, you're still a solid member of the sedentary set, full of good in-

Waistline

To whittle down your waistline, try this twist.
Sit down, with your legs straight in front of
you as wide apart as you can. Clasp your hand
behind your neck, keeping your back straight a
erect. Then bend forward, and try to touch you
left knee with your right elbow. Straighten up,
and touch your right knee with your left elbow.

tentions but somehow never carrying them out, the very idea of exercise may trigger off uncomfortable pangs of guilt. Even worse, it may conjure up all sorts of grim visions: exhausting workouts in a jungle of complicated equipment; hectic follow-the-leader sessions with some TV gymnast; all-weather joggers who get up at dawn to race through the park; or a gaggle of miserable ladies huffing and puffing to the music of a tinny piano.

If "exercise" sends bleak visions like this dancing through your head, it's hardly surprising if you've shied away from it so far. But does it have to be like this? Decidedly not, though a certain percentage of the nation's 40 million exercisers—and that includes the men as well as the women—actually seem to enjoy punishing themselves a little. Maybe it's just the Puritan in them coming out: "If it hurts, it must be good for you."

By and large, however, it's the fitness fanatics who tend to take this tack. When they get the exercising bug they get it bad, and usually can't wait to tell the world how they're beating themselves into good health. With them, it's all aches and pains, sweat and tears; but, as you may have noticed, the more noise they make about it, the sooner

Waistline

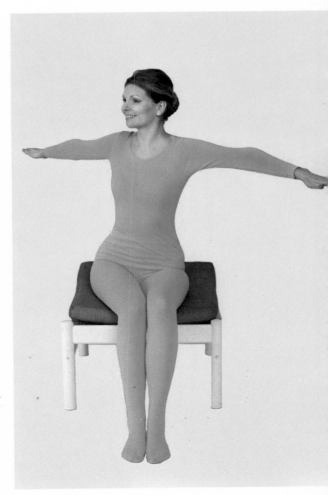

they always seem to throw in the towel.

The faddists' mistake lies in being over-ambitious. They approach exercise as they would approach a crash diet: immediate success guaranteed if they devote themselves to it body and soul for a few short weeks.

The real secret of exercising—like the real secret of dieting—is all contained in the simple phrase, "Slow but sure." What few people realize is that every muscle in our bodies is both highly responsive and quietly resistant. Though each will always try to do your bidding, it can only become capable of really new things by changing slowly, at its own steady pace. But change it will, so long as you do. Linda Clark, author of *Stay Young Longer*, makes this crystal clear: "If you contract a muscle for only a few seconds, and perform it once every day; you can re-condition, tone, and improve that muscle 4 per cent in a week and 50 per cent in 12 weeks."

So obviously, there's no point in torturing your body with a violent crash program of exercise. The agonizing aches and pains you'll experience will just be your muscles complaining that you are asking too much too soon. Far more serious, you might be putting yourself in real danger. It cannot be

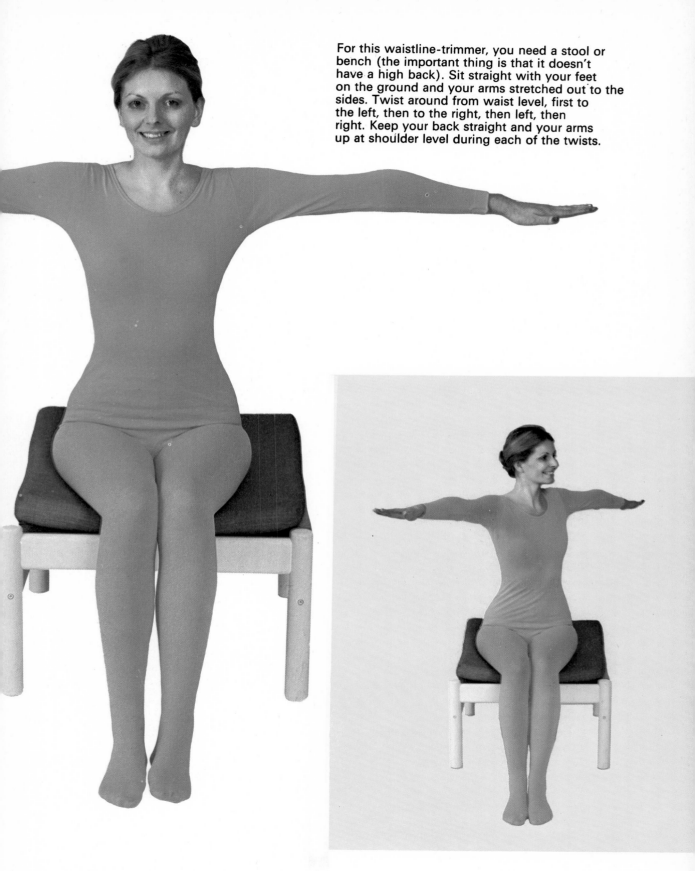

For this waistline-trimmer, you need a stool or bench (the important thing is that it doesn't have a high back). Sit straight with your feet on the ground and your arms stretched out to the sides. Twist around from waist level, first to the left, then to the right, then left, then right. Keep your back straight and your arms up at shoulder level during each of the twists.

Abdomen

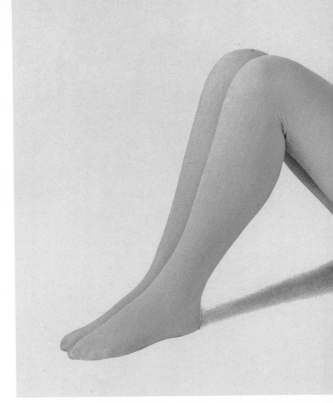

The best girdle for your tummy is your own muscles. Strengthen them this way: lie flat on the floor on your back, with your arms stretched out above your head, and your knees relaxed. Keep your soles on the floor. Now try to raise your hips up off the floor while you pull in your abdomen muscles. Take it easy until you get used to the exercise.

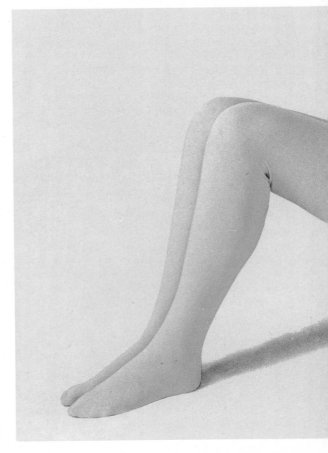

stressed too strongly that the more sedentary the life you've been leading—particularly if you're over 30—the more imperative it is to seek the advice of a doctor before beginning even the most moderate exercise program.

Assuming that you do have your doctor's approval, what's the best way to start? You can't do better than to follow the advice of fitness expert Bonnie Pruden: "Substitute activity for inactivity as much as you can in the course of a normal day," she says. For example, count up the hours you usually spend sitting down, and resolve to reduce them. Try doing things in a more old-fashioned way; all those extra little efforts your mother had to make added up to a kind of mini exercise program in themselves. Try to stop pushing buttons—whether they be for the toothbrush, the can opener, the blender, the floor waxer, the automatic car wash, or whatever. Electricity, bless its insidious little heart, is an enemy.

As Bonnie Pruden suggests, "Give up trying to make life less physical and make it more physical. Call up your friends and invite them to meet you after dinner for a walk.

If you always take the elevator, start walking the last flight. Every two weeks, add one more floor that you walk. If you're a commuter, walk to the station. Don't drive your children everywhere; make them walk." (And walk with them.)

After a few weeks of consciously putting more natural energy into your life, you'll begin to feel like trying your hand at a more demanding form of exercise. In fact, you'll have increased your appetite for activity. When you reach this delightful stage, the door swings wide open, and you have a tremendous range of exercises, sports, and activities to choose from. How do you decide which ones are right for you?

Here, there's no pat answer. Even the experts don't agree. It's been said, and wisely, that exercise needs are as individualistic as fingerprints. They can vary according to a woman's age and state of health, her weight and figure problems, her tastes and temperament. In fact, it's for this very reason that so many different exercise schemes have been developed.

Basically, they all fit into two main categories. The first, generally called *aerobics,* includes a variety of informal activities which, if done regularly and in easy stages, can do wonders to improve your general health, fitness, and allover firmness. They include jogging, swimming, bicycling, jumping rope, dancing, and brisk walking. Each raises your pulse rate above normal and keeps it there at a steady level for short, prescribed periods of time while a fresh supply of oxygen pumps through your system. Each revitalizes the heart/lung process, and noticeably improves your general feeling of well-being.

Obviously, all of these activities require a fair amount of energy expenditure, and none of them should be started without first consulting a doctor. The idea is to build up your body's reserves of energy and stamina slowly. With jogging, for example, the best way to start is by alternating 30 seconds each of running and walking, and for only five minutes at a time. Jumping rope—just as you did as a child, and to those good old

Hips

If you sit a lot, you may be wider across the hips than you'd like. Try this to slim them down: sit on the floor with your legs straight in front of you, feet apart. Lean back on your hands. Now, pointing your toes down, swing your left leg over to the other side of your right leg, trying to touch the floor with your toe. Then swing your right leg over. Get a smooth rolling motion so that your hips move with your legs. Be sure to return to starting position after each separate swing to the sides.

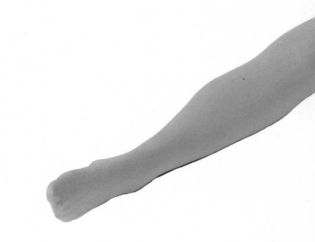

childhood rhymes if you like—should also be done for just five minutes at a time to begin with. It helps if you use a rope with swivel handles.

Many a woman still flinches at the idea of doing anything so obvious. Who can blame her, if her choice is limited to the park or to the floor above irritable neighbors. In any case, if she wants to do something vigorous, beneficial, and informal, she has several other choices. One of these is bicycling, which has soared in popularity over the past few years. A bike makes an excellent substitute for a car. You can use it whenever you need to go down to the store for something you've forgotten, or when you're on

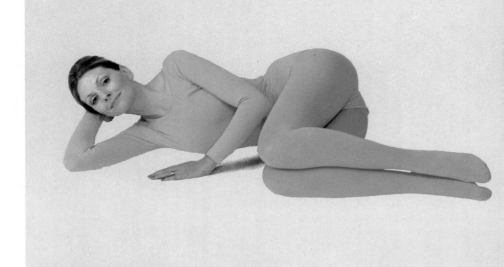

Hips

Another hip improver. Lie on your side, resting your head on one arm and use the other for balance. Bring both knees up to your chest, then stretch one out parallel to the floor as far as you can, then tuck it up again. Stretch the other leg. Try to do this one as rapidly as possible, keeping your hips still.

your way over to a friend's for coffee. By leaving the car in the garage, you're not only doing your body a favor, but are also reducing air pollution.

Swimming, by general agreement, is the best exercise for toning up and strengthening every muscle you have. Both Katherine Hepburn and Rose Kennedy are lifelong advocates of swimming—and look at them.

Anything that gets your legs moving will benefit your entire system. Dancing—no matter what type, provided it's done regularly—has this effect. Have you ever seen a professional dancer, male or female, who wasn't trim and full of vitality? Taking long, brisk walks—breathing in and out deeply and rhythmically as you stride along—is a superb way to improve fitness and muscle tone. Many people have rediscovered the

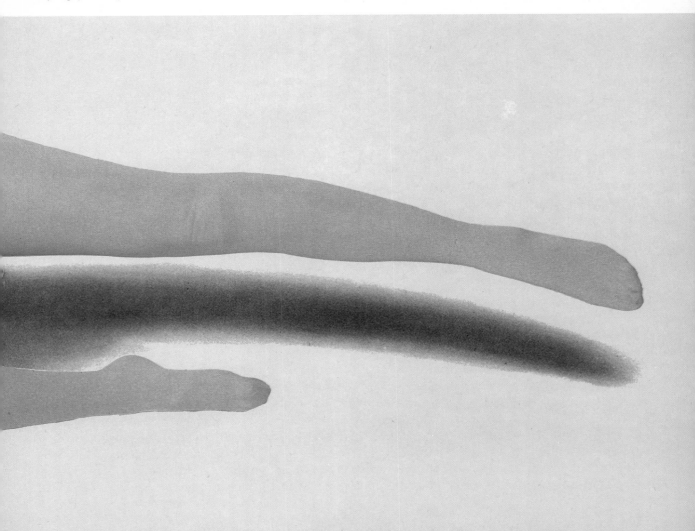

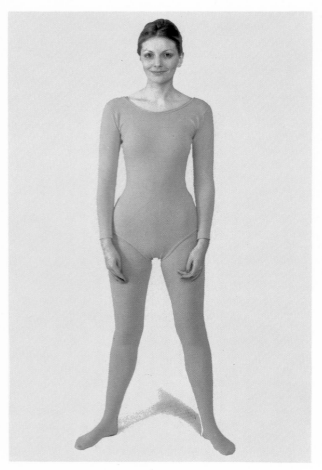

Thighs

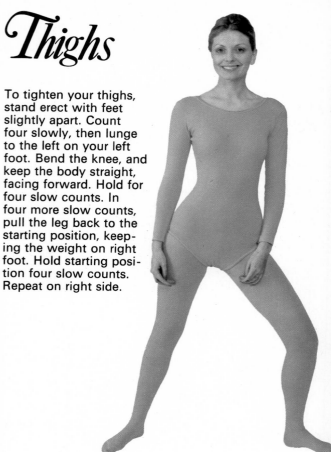

To tighten your thighs, stand erect with feet slightly apart. Count four slowly, then lunge to the left on your left foot. Bend the knee, and keep the body straight, facing forward. Hold for four slow counts. In four more slow counts, pull the leg back to the starting position, keeping the weight on right foot. Hold starting position four slow counts. Repeat on right side.

true meaning of the old-fashioned word "constitutional." It can be done safely at any age, and, if your caloric intake remains the same, a daily one-mile walk can leave you 10 pounds lighter at the end of a year.

Into the second major category of exercises fall all the special programs designed to improve specific figure problems. Many of them not only tone and trim particular areas, but also improve general fitness as well. They range all the way from isometrics and isotonics to gymnastics and calisthenics. Don't let all this terminology scare you; they're all pretty uncomplicated.

Isometrics are any exercises that pit one muscle against another. They enjoyed a great vogue a few years ago, but have now more or less gone out of fashion—at least for women—because they tend to develop, rather than simply tone up muscles. But there is one isometric exercise every woman

can use to advantage: the one designed to tone and lighten the pectoral muscles above and around the breasts. Simply grasp both arms just below the elbow and, without sliding your hands, push upward as hard as you can for a few seconds. Done once or twice a day, this exercise can do a lot to help your breasts resist the pull of gravity over the years.

Isotonics are exercises that simply stretch or contract certain muscles to give them tone and flexibility. Broadly speaking, isotonics include yoga, especially the modern, simplified versions advocated by experts like Eve Diskin and Richard Hittleman; Tai-Chi, the newly fashionable Chinese exercises; and the Mensendieck System, which originated before World War I, but is only now beginning to catch on. All three are particularly good forms of exercise because they combine minimum strain with

More thigh work. Stand erect with your hands on your hips and heels together. Rise up on your toes and then slowly squat. Return slowly to original position. (Try using the back of a chair to balance until you get used to this.)

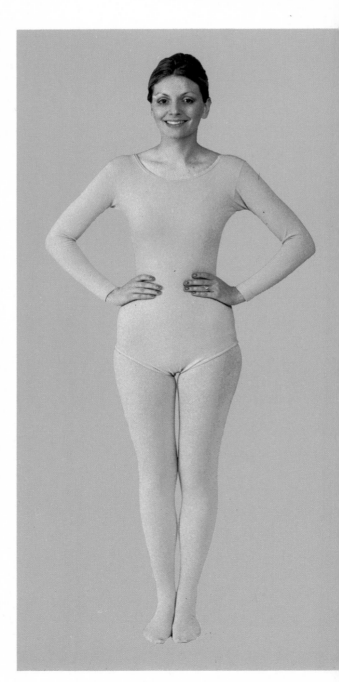

maximum results. All three have a way of looking like child's play. They're not, of course, and to be fully effective, they should first be practiced with an instructor.

Yoga's popularity—and it is amazingly popular these days—rests on its ability to benefit both mind and body. Through it, you not only learn how to firm and limber up long disused muscles, but also how to relax, and how to breathe so as to nourish every part of your body.

Tai-Chi, though as ancient as China itself, is a fairly new wrinkle on the U.S. exercise scene. It consists of a succession of slow but disciplined movements designed to tone your muscles, stimulate your circulation, and calm your nerves.

The Mensendieck System, created by Dr. Bess Mensendieck 50 years ago, is based on the simple premise that by learning to do normal body movements, such as walking, bending, stretching, reaching and sitting, in the proper way, anyone can train themselves to be as naturally fit and supple as a cat— and for the same reasons. Nature never intended us to be awkward or bulgy. We simply get that way through years of in-activity and self-neglect. The Mensendieck approach certainly makes sense, but, like yoga and Tai-Chi, requires instruction.

Gymnastics are simply exercises done with special apparatus—the kind you find in a gym. Unless you're training to be an athlete, they're better left to the men.

Calisthenics, on the other hand, require no special equipment, and are chiefly designed with women in mind. They include a wide variety of programs. Among them are the celebrated Royal Canadian Air Force Exer-

cise Plans; early morning classes offered on TV (millions of women swear by these daily video sessions); the excellent "Keep Fit" and "Maid-to-Measure" courses offered by the YWCA; and the highly personalized, but rather expensive, classes offered by figure experts such as Marjorie Craig, Nick Kounovsky, and Jan Cameron.

What so many women like about the calisthenic type of exercise program is that it can be precisely geared to particular figure problems. They also like the companionship and authority provided by an instructor who tells them exactly what exercises to do, how long to do them, and which muscles they'll affect. In fact, what could be better?

Perhaps, however, for various reasons, you'd like to try going it alone. There's something to be said for gradually improving the way you look and feel without anyone knowing what you're up to. By the same token, if nobody knows you're doing it, there's nobody around to keep you at it, so you'll need a bit of self-discipline.

One way to substantially increase your chances of success is to think of your own exercise program as a sort of secret vice, something you can tell no one about. The aura of "forbidden fruit" makes anything more fun—and more irresistible. Little by little, your own quiet daily dozen will be helping you achieve that cherished goal of a trim, firm and supple figure.

This kind of exercise doesn't have to be a big deal. It doesn't have to be tiring, painful, or boring. In fact, it can and should be just the opposite: a golden opportunity to do something positive for yourself that not only

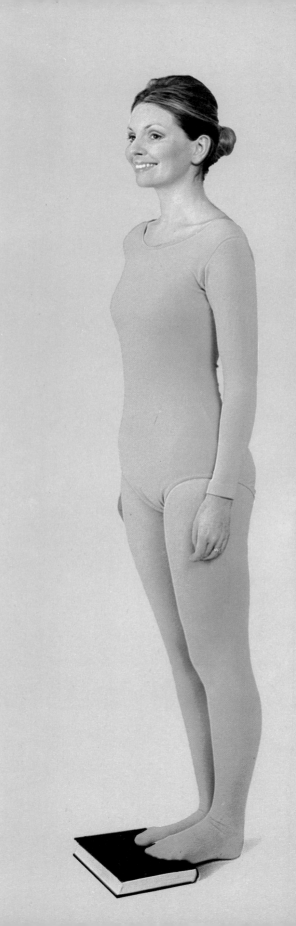

112

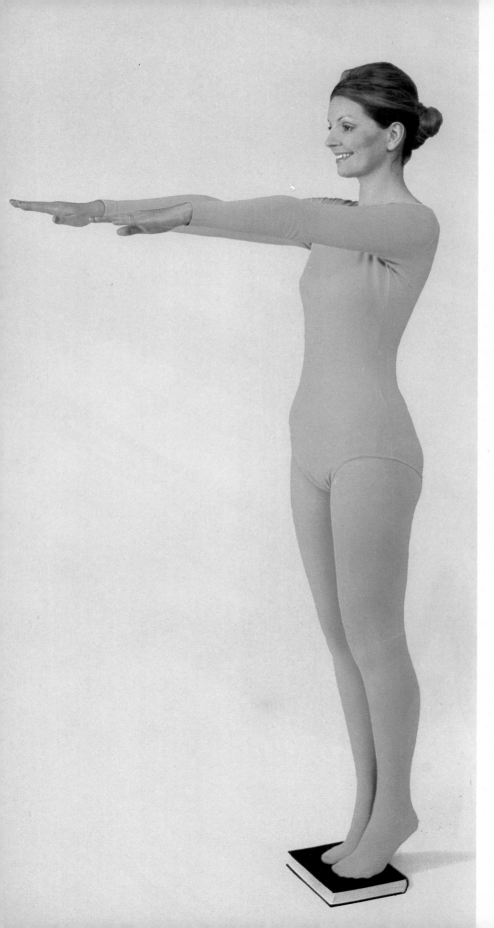

Calves

For this exercise for your calves you need a book about an inch thick. Stand straight with your toes and the balls of your feet on the book, your heels on the floor. Raise your heels off the floor, breathe in at the count of one and raise your arms to shoulder level, going up and up to the count of five. Then go down slowly, returning to starting position. As you get used to this exercise use thicker and thicker books until you get to one three inches thick.

Ankles

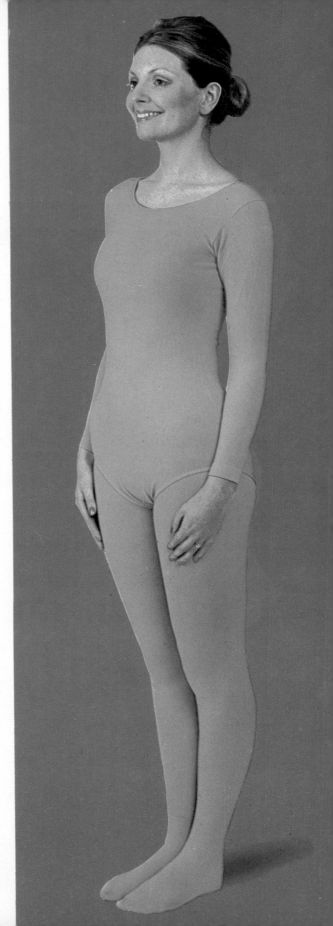

adds substantially to your attractiveness, but also makes you feel more vital and alive. The best part of all is that it only takes 10 minutes a day to keep you in the pink, whatever your age.

The key words, of course, are "every day." Most of us, at some time or other, have resolved to start exercising; and have carried out our good intentions for at least a week or so before giving up. We provide ourselves with all sorts of excuses: not enough time, not enough energy, or, perhaps, not enough of that once much-admired virtue, will power. We all know, of course, that exercises have to be done daily and over a long period of time to produce the results we want, but we have the unfortunate tendency to regard them as some kind of chore or duty. Let's dispense with that whole dreary view, here and now, and give exercise its due. It is in fact a positive luxury, with delightfully cumulative benefits—as you'll see for yourself after only a few weeks.

How should you begin? First, pick the 10 minutes that you know you can give yourself every day—while you wait for the kids to come down for breakfast, perhaps, or for your husband to come home from work. Maybe the best time for you is halfway through the day, as a refreshing break from

114

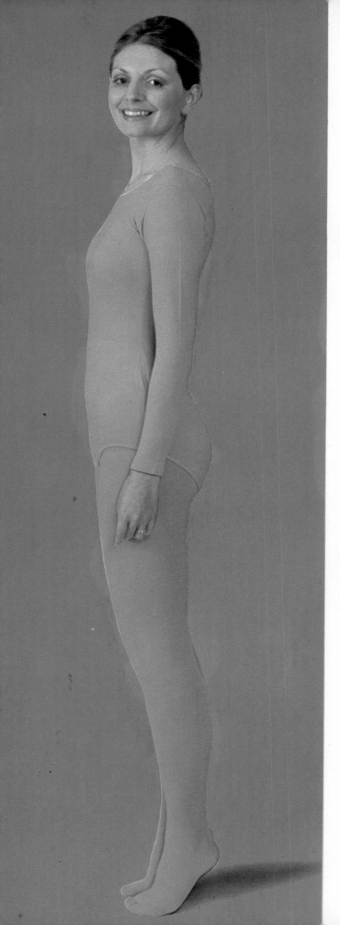

Tired of thick ankles?
Try this: stand straight
with your feet flat on
the floor. Raise your
heels until you are
standing high on your
toes and then slap! snap
your heels back to floor.

your housework. Then, make yourself comfortable, and, if you can, exercise to music, the more rhythmic the better. Above all, don't strain yourself; the whole point is to feel truly refreshed and more relaxed after gently stretching and toning your muscles.

There are, of course, literally hundreds of exercise books available. But to help you get started, we've illustrated, throughout this chapter, some of the best and most effective exercises for different parts of the body. Start by doing the ones that you want, and like, only a few times each, and gradually work up to more. You'll be surprised at how soon you can—and easily, too.

The greatest blessings any form of exercise can bestow are good health and good looks. Hand in hand with both go gracefulness and good posture. A woman who carries herself well and moves fluidly can turn every head at a party, simply because her calm, self-assured bearing announces quietly but firmly, "I am not afraid. I like being me, and I know that you will like me too."

Exercise can improve your posture, give you a trimmer and more supple figure, and —yes—bring you a greater measure of serenity by releasing muscular tension. You will actually feel lighter and more graceful as a result of exercising—and, it will show.

Getting it all Together

8

Not so long ago, the words "high fashion" were fraught with all the solemn authority of a latter-day Commandment. The fashion designers issued their decrees, the manufacturers carried them out, and overnight, a new look was born. Women everywhere took it seriously, and did their level best to like it and copy it—whether or not it flattered their figures or suited their personalities.

True, changing fashions suited different tastes and figures at different times, but never all women at once. Each style seemed to be geared for just one ideal type. You had to be practically hipless and bosomless, for example, to wear the soft, smooth lines of the 1920's and 30's, and then progressively more well-endowed for the sweater girl look of the 1940's and the hourglass silhouette of the 50's.

The fashion pendulum swung back and forth, but there was always "a shape," "a look," and a definite set of fashion rules to follow. This was still true during the early 1960's, when the last word in elegance was the kind of slender, ultra-simple outfits that Jackie Kennedy wore to perfection.

And then, POW! the whole scene was turned topsy-turvy and shaken to its foundations. Suddenly, fashion ideas began to work their way up from—not down to—the average Miss and Mrs., and it became "do your own thing" from London to Los Angeles. Chiefly, of course, it was the young who actually did their own thing—rum-

The 1970's may easily be the best time in history for fashion, simply because women don't have to live up to any rigid rules or set styles. How pleasantly different from the decades of the 30's, 40's, 50's and 60's, when fashion dictated what you wore, whether or not it was flattering to you.

maging around at the Salvation Army and secondhand shops for Civil War, Victorian, Army, and other new types of gear. They had their effect, too: an entirely new sense of fun and freedom was injected into the whole idea of fashion. As one writer put it, "Fashion is dead. Long live clothes!"

This revolution has by no means toppled the fashion industry. Its real impact has been more like a revelation—opening everyone's eyes to the possibilities of many different shapes and looks. In fact, the fashion industry has been quick to answer the call for more variety, and has come up with a broader range of choice than anyone would have dreamed possible. Now, for the first time, we all have a chance to experiment, to use wit and imagination where clothing is concerned.

Gone are the days when the social occasion dictated precisely what to wear. Gone is the time when a skirt just an inch too long or too short actually felt wrong against your leg. And gone too, happily, is the era when your age determined exactly which department you headed for when you entered a store. The single fashion rule today is: dress to suit *your* shape, *your* personality, and *your* lifestyle.

Naturally, with all this freedom, there are bound to be times when you feel you simply can't decide what to wear, when or where. You may even find yourself wishing for the good old days, when the rules were clear-cut. If so, you'll be wishing away a precious opportunity to discover exactly what looks best on you. It might prove as simple as the classic shirtwaist, or little black dress. Or as sporty as a well-fitting pair of blue jeans. Or as elegant as a beautifully tailored pants suit. Or as exotic as an embroidered kaftan

We all have clothes that could be reshaped for a second life to enlarge our wardrobe. Try this with a shrunken, ordinary pullover sweater. Cut off the sleeves and lower the neck, binding with a bright braid. Use your new jerkin over a blouse or over another sweater.

or African dashiki. The basic thing to remember is that now is *your* moment. Use clothes to enhance your individuality, and your own special assets.

There are some good guidelines you can follow to bring out your best features and camouflage those you are less happy about. More about them later. Right now, the first thing to tackle—if you haven't done it already—is your closet. No one can go far with a wardrobe full of the flotsam and jetsam of bygone days. This is especially true if the flotsam and jetsam includes things that need cleaning or mending, and dated items you've kept only because you thought you could do something with them someday.

Haul everything out of your closet and have a look at it. The same goes for your drawers. Make three piles: the good (your all-time favorites); the bad (potential goodies that are languishing for lack of a quick stitch or the attention of the cleaners); and the ugly (those beyond hope—we all have a few lurking in the depths of closets or drawers).

Without further ado, pack up your uglies —any badly battered shoes, outmoded or unflattering skirts and dresses, worn-out pants, shirts, and sweaters—and send them to a local church, the Salvation Army, or the nearest thrift shop.

Then tackle your potential goodies. Dispatch rumpled clothes to the cleaners, run-down shoes to the shoemakers. Get out a needle and thread and attend to any sagging hems, open seams, and loose buttons. Finish up by ironing anything that needs it. If by the way, you simply hate sewing and ironing, find yourself a dependable dry cleaner that does alterations as well, and, in future, avoid

clothes that are extra fussy or wrinkle prone.

By now you should be feeling most virtuous. Just weeding out and revitalizing the clothes you already have acts like a tonic. To complete your sense of well-being, roll up your sleeves and clean, spray paint, or reline your drawers and closet before putting everything away. It might help, too, to invest in a couple of space-savers—things like multi-

Your spring dress-and-coat set is probably languishing at the back of your closet where it's been for a year or more. Bring it up to date by shortening the dress and wearing it as a tunic over a pair of trousers, with the coat as it is.

If your trusty A-line dress seems a bit too short these days, try wearing it over a pair of trousers. Give your whole appearance a new look by wearing a head scarf that tones with the color of the pants.

tiered skirt and shirt hangers, and a roomy shoe rack for the bottom of your closet. Another good idea is to compartmentalize your drawers with strips of cardboard wedged in as dividers at strategic points. This ensures a certain amount of order in the inevitable chaos of tights and lingerie. Be sure, also, to outfit your closet with a clothes bag large enough to hold all your most

fragile things. There's nothing worse than discovering that the soft dress or blouse you really loved has been irreparably damaged by the rough buckle of the coat hanging next to it.

Everything stashed away with loving care? Now stand back and feel proud. You know what you've got, and you know it's well cared for. You're now ready to make some addi-

Bras come in hundreds of different styles, and each is designed for a specific job. The one on the left, with an unseamed cup, gives a smooth natural look under sweaters. In the center, the bra has a wired undercup to give a more defined shape. The bra on the right is for dramatic dresses when you want cleavage to show. The bra lifts your breasts gently, separating the bosom. When you choose your next bra, decide what you want to wear that particular bra with, and consult with the lingerie salesgirl—she'll know how to guide you and help you get exactly the right fit.

tions. Of course, it's a rare bird who can go out and fill up the gaps in her wardrobe all at once. Besides, who'd want to? Half the fun of having clothes lies in the gradual accumulation of them, "find" by "find".

Now for some shopping tips. First of all, buy with your present wardrobe in mind. Curb the impulse to buy something—a pair of shoes, a belt or a jacket, for example—that wouldn't go with anything you already have. What you want is a complementary whole, not an assortment of pieces that don't fit together. Think in terms of mix and match; even the smallest wardrobe then has terrific possibilities if the separate parts are interchangeable. This, of course, means getting colors and textures that go together.

Discover the colors that suit you best, and then vary their shades. This doesn't mean you should get hung up on any one color family; "navy blue people" get known as "navy blue people." It does everyone good to try something completely different once in a while. Keep an open mind, and don't automatically reject certain colors or color combinations merely because you've never worn them before. Who knows, maybe that deep wine, lush brown, shocking pink, or sunshine yellow has always been right for you—only you didn't know it! Remember, too, that a splash of color—a bright scarf or an eye-catching belt, for example—can do wonders to perk up a dark or muted outfit.

Other buying tips: when you find something you really like, something that flatters you and makes you feel like a million, buy it, even if you don't much need it at the

Below: these three clever ads for Ohrbach's department store in New York hilariously demonstrate what can happen when a woman lets fashion run away with her. Now look at the three women above the ads. They're the same age, and have the same basic figures as Ohrbach's "bad examples" —but what a difference!

Left: a soft wool pant-suit with a long tunic top does a visual slimming job for this model. The total effect is a far cry from the over-stuffed look shown below. Right: crisp and contemporary, this shirtdress typifies the cool elegance any woman can have, provided her clothes not only fit, but suit her.

Is the wrong person wearing the pants in your family?

Liberated ladies, don't get upset. Ohrbach's is definitely not opposed to pants for women. And if you need any proof of that, just pop into one of our stores, where you'll always find an exciting selection of styles, colors and sizes.

But we don't think pants are right for everybody. Nor is everybody right for pants. And the same holds true for every style that was ever designed.

That's why Ohrbach's stores are filled with so many thousands of fashions. We know that with so much to choose from, you're sure to find the look that's just right for you. At a price that's just right for your pocketbook.

So if you're not sure whether to wear pants or not, come in and try on a pair.
See how you look from the front.
See how you look from the side.
And then, as a final favor to yourself and the rest of us, see how you look from the rear.

OHRBACH'S Where you always find the fashion and the price that's right for you.

It's in, but maybe you shouldn't be in it.

Some girls look sensational in hot pants. Front, back and sideways. So for those gorgeous girls Ohrbach's has an assortment of stylish hot pants and warm pants. All at Ohrbach's fabulously low prices.

But no one style is right for everybody. And a girl who looks absolutely divine in one outfit can look positively dreadful in another.

That's why Ohrbach's has so many thousands of fashions to choose from. We know there's a right look for everyone, and when you come into our store we want to be sure that it isn't right if it isn't right for you.

you'll find the one that's right for you. And at a price you can afford. At Ohrbach's, we believe

OHRBACH'S Where you always find the right fashion and the price that's right for you.

Right: what could be more "with it" than this sporty checked suit? This is a perfect example of dressing your age without looking like a dowager queen. The woman below certainly has the figure for the latest gear, but on her it looks all wrong somehow. True fashion sense, as always, is flattering the woman you are.

moment. When you need it, you won't be able to find it again. The same goes for those special treasurers, bras and girdles that fit like a dream, or pants and shirts that are exactly right for you. When you find them, buy yourself more than one. There's nothing more annoying than finding that a manufacturer has discontinued a certain line, just when you want to buy more of it.

Hunt around for a shop that sells your kind of clothes, and if possible, go there when it's least crowded. If you should find a sympathetic and inspired salesgirl, stick by her—she's worth her weight in gold. Last but not least, take your time when you're purchasing things. Sit down in them, walk around in them, bend over in them. Clothes should fit to perfection—but not to the kind of perfection that requires the rigid stance of a marine. You are not a still life, but a woman in motion, and your clothes should move comfortably with you, touching, but not binding or squeezing your body. Nor should they contradict your own inner style. Clothes are but an extension of your own individuality, and should never be allowed to dominate the person inside them. As Coco Chanel once put it, "Look for the woman in the dress. If there is no woman, there is no dress."

What about the woman under the dress? Next to her skin she's wearing something that is fully as important as her dress—lingerie. When you come right down to it, there's nothing like the secret knowledge that you're wearing pretty underwear to make you feel great. It may not be such a secret, either. Besides your husband, there's your doctor, and the other women in the communal dressing rooms of modern boutiques to see what you've got on underneath.

Take the plunge and buy yourself something downright luxurious. Also have at least one bra, slip, pair of pants, or girdle that isn't white. Try black, beige, or a splashy print to give your morale a boost.

While we're on the subject, take the time and spend the money to get properly fitting bras, girdles, and foundation garments. Don't be embarrassed to ask for the advice and assistance of a saleswoman in the lingerie department. She's seen hundreds of other women and knows more than you ever will about how to suit the garment to the figure. Neither bra nor girdle should be too tight—if they are, they'll create bulges above and below, where they cut into the flesh. Don't ever wear extra-strong girdles. A little too much support is a dangerous thing. It encourages the abdominal muscles to give up and go to sleep. Ideally, you shouldn't rely too much on a girdle or foundation garment to control your curves, but they can be useful for added support and increased smoothness of line.

Another fundamental item you should take care in choosing is your shoes. No matter how fashionable they are, ill-fitting shoes—or boots—are vicious enemies. You don't break *them* in; they break *you* in, and put your feet through all kinds of terrible tortures in the meantime. Mid-afternoon is a good time to buy shoes, because that's when your feet are likely to be at their biggest. (Everyone's feet go through slight variations in size during the day.) If you have especially hard-to-fit feet—extra broad, long, or narrow—shop around until you find the kind of shoes and boots that not only look good, but feel good.

Now for those general guidelines we promised on how to flatter your own particular figure. They break down into three simple things to watch for and experiment with: texture, color, and line.

First, texture. The essential point to remember is that any thick, shaggy, or nubby material markedly adds bulk to your figure. If you're tall and slim, you might welcome the extra body provided by heavy wools, bulky knits, fun furs, and strong-surfaced

The coordinated look no longer means dressing in the same color from top to bottom, but it still means avoiding a clash of colors. More, it means that make-up should be a part of your outfit—your hair, your eyes, your mouth, and your hands all part of the color coordination. To use this chart, decide which outfit colors you want to wear. Across from that outfit, in the line after your own hair color, you find the coordinated make-up colors.

fabrics like corduroy and seersucker. If you're not, beware—unless you're aiming for the round and cuddly look. The shorter and fuller your figure, the more you should seek out smooth-finished fabrics like jersey, soft wool, gabardine, linen, and cotton. A final point: shiny materials like rayon, silk, vinyl, and patent leather can have an enlarging effect because they pick up the light and draw attention to prominent features—your hips or bosom, perhaps, or, in the case of patent leather, your feet.

Second, color. Like shiny surfaces, color creates purely optical effects. Used imaginatively, it can do almost anything you want it to do. There are just three things to bear in mind. One: dark colors tend to diminish and de-emphasize a figure, while bright, clear tones tend to enlarge and emphasize it. Two: one-color outfits have a slenderizing effect, while multicolor clothes—bold prints, patterns, and plaids, for example—increase the illusion of width. Three: vertical lines of color add height to a figure, while horizontal color contrasts—particularly at the waist—tend to chop up a figure, and shorten it.

Now for some examples. Supposing, first of all, that you're tall and rather thin. Bright colors and bold patterns are for you. Not only can you carry them off with style, but also you can use them strategically to diminish the effect of height. Broad bands of color that carry the eye from side to side, rather than up and down, or a definite color contrast at the waist—a white shirt with a plum colored skirt, for example—will help break up the long slim line.

If you're on the short side, whether plump or slender, or if you're tall but heavy, try to avoid large patterns and horizontal color

Outfit Color	Hair	EYE SHADOW	LIGHT SKIN	DARK SKIN	LIPSTICK	NAILS
	Black					
	Auburn					
	Mid Brown					
	Blonde					
	Silver					
	Black					
	Auburn					
	Mid Brown					
	Blonde					
	Silver					
	Black					
	Auburn					
	Mid Brown					
	Blonde					
	Silver					
	Black					
	Auburn					
	Mid Brown					
	Blonde					
	Silver					

contrasts. They have a widening effect on already well-endowed women, and a diminishing effect on short ones. Your best bet is one-piece, one-color clothes. The smooth flow of color from shoulder to hem, or from shoulder to ankle, if it's a maxi style or pants suit, will make you look slimmer and taller.

The cagey use of color is especially important where tights and stockings are concerned. If you have pencil-slim legs, then by all means wear white and patterned stockings. If your legs tend to be a bit heavy, though, tights or stockings the color of your skin or a bit darker will be much more flattering.

Line is perhaps the most crucial element in any clothing. You've already seen how color can be used to give the illusion of height and width. Line operates in much the same way, but with far greater subtlety. Line is at work everywhere in an article of clothing, from its basic shape (full or tapered), to its distinguishing characteristics (hemline, neckline, waistline, and sleeve length), to its finer details (tucks, seams, buttons, zipper, belt, or pockets). Each plays a part in accentuating or de-emphasizing figure pluses and minuses.

As a general rule, the more vertical the line, the more heightening the effect. This is especially true at eye-catching points such as the shoulders, bosom, waist, and hips. Thus, for example, V-necks and long necklaces, long vests and tunics, overblouses and long, loose sleeves, A-line and empire style dresses all tend to draw the eye up and down, and increase the illusion of height and slenderness. Conversely, boatnecks and smocking, short or puffed sleeves, shirts tucked into skirts or pants, belts worn at hip level, flared jackets, and mid-calf boots tend to break up the line and send the eye zigzagging across the figure, adding to the impression of width. As always, however, the rules were made to be broken, and you can never tell just which combination of factors—and that includes line, color, and texture—will do most for you till you give it a try. So experiment a little.

One thing we haven't touched on as yet is

Your beauty remains what it was all along—you, as your best, happy, and confident self. There will be days when you feel less than happy or confident, and you may find, as many women do, that on those days, taking special care with your clothes and make-up gives an unexplainable lift to spirits. The techniques in this book are for your own enjoyment. Have a beautiful time experimenting!

accessories. There was a time when they were all-important, and color-matched sets of hat and gloves, shoes and handbag could be found in every woman's wardrobe. Not any more. The idea now—and it makes sense—is to highlight your outfit with one key accessory, a bright scarf, an unusual pin, belt or handbag. One bold accent gives the eye something to focus on, and adds sparkle to whatever you're wearing.

Try to make the most of your every asset, whether it be a swanlike neck or a well-defined waist, pretty shoulders or a neat ankle, a fine bosom or a firm, round bottom. If your figure is fuller than you'd like, for example, there's no reason why you should go around in a tent. You've got curves that many a skinny woman would envy; don't hide them away.

You may find, on examining yourself carefully, that you've been busy camouflaging what you consider to be your bad points for so long that you've entirely overlooked your assets. Now's the time to discover and enhance them with clothes that proudly tell the world who you are.

You may also find that it takes more time to get something just right for you than it does to buy one of the many repetitious articles on the racks of every department store. Don't be put off. Spend the necessary time. It pays off in the sheer pleasure of wearing something that suits you right down to the ground, makes you feel wonderful, and turns heads wherever you go.

Finally, always remember that the person inside the clothes—yourself—is special and unique. Cherish yourself, and above all, perfect the art of dressing to show your own, individual womanliness.

Right: British singer Cilla Black, after her well-publicized nose operation in 1969. A childhood accident had left her with slight breathing difficulties, and it was this, she said, that finally decided her on having her nose resculpted. Below: the "old" Cilla.

128

Questions and Answers about Cosmetic Surgery

Is there anyone these days who isn't fascinated by the possibilities of cosmetic surgery? Whether or not you'd ever dream of it for yourself, it's hard to ignore the enthusiastic claims being made for it. Not to be ignored either, is the simple but astonishing fact of its growth in popularity. In 1949, a mere 15,000 men and women underwent cosmetic surgery. By 1969, the figure had soared to 500,000. Who's having it done? Not, as you might imagine, only the rich and famous. Today, the candidate for cosmetic surgery is just as likely to be a housewife as an actress, a salesman as a politician, a secretary as a darling of the jet set. More surprising still, his or her income may not top $9,000 a year.

The communications media have been quick to seize on the newsmaking potential of this trend, and are busily publicizing cosmetic surgery as a fountain of youth and beauty for everyone. It's as simple as ABC, they tell us. Irregular features can be corrected, wrinkles and acne scars erased, sagging faces lifted, breasts made larger or smaller, arms, legs, and bottoms reduced. Sensational! Change your looks to suit your wishes. Simply ask and it shall be granted—provided you can pay, of course.

Is it really this simple, though? Despite the publicity it receives, cosmetic surgery remains a mystery to most of us. Exactly what can it achieve? What are its limitations? Precisely how and where is it done? Is it dangerous in any way? Does it leave scars? How much does it cost? What psychological effects can it have? How noticeable are the results of such surgery to other people?

The following pages are devoted to answering these and other questions about this controversial new aspect of beauty. Our aim is to provide the facts—and just as many of them as we can fit in. So, fasten your seat belts. We'll start out with the kinds of general questions that apply to all types of cosmetic surgery, then cover the details of specific operations: from "nose jobs" to ear corrections, facelifts to chemical "peels" breast implants to the various types of "body lifts."

Some General Questions

Why this big upsurge in cosmetic surgery? Is it a brand-new science?

Not at all. It started at least 2,000 years ago, when Hindu surgeons began using skin grafts to repair damaged ears and noses. This kind of surgery remained very much in its infancy, however, until the terrible wars and new weapons of this century. Suddenly, surgeons everywhere were faced with a desperate challenge: thousands of young soldiers urgently needed reconstructive plastic surgery. The techniques devised to meet this challenge went on developing in peacetime, and were used to help the victims of accident and disease, as well as the many unhappy children born with severe physical defects.

It wasn't long before plastic surgeons were also being asked to operate on healthy individuals with minor abnormalities of face or figure, or early and unwanted signs of age. Today, many plastic surgeons perform both reconstructive operations—to restore or create normal appearance—and purely cosmetic operations—to enhance or improve normal appearance. Perhaps the chief distinction between the two types of surgery is that the first is usually suggested by the doctor or hospital, while the second is suggested by the patient himself.

How many plastic surgeons are there?

There are about 1,200 such surgeons scattered across the United States. Most towns with over 100,000 inhabitants have at least one, and the big cities, of course, have many more. There are also a lot of quacks around—some of them doctors unqualified to practice plastic surgery, others merely self-styled "aestheticians" with no medical qualifications whatsoever.

How do you find one you can trust?

Beware of any plastic surgeon who advertizes, and don't go by word-of-mouth recommendations. The best way to select a plastic surgeon is to contact the medical profession itself. You can write or phone the Specialist Referral Board of your County Medical Society, and ask for a list of accredited plastic surgeons in your area. Or you can go to the local library and consult a directory of qualified medical specialists under the heading "Plastic Surgery," picking a few names from those practicing in your area. Or you can write to the American Medical Association, 535 North Dearborn Street, Chicago, Illinois 60610, for their list of accredited plastic surgeons, again selecting a few names from those near your home. Or you can write directly to the Secretary of the American Board of Plastic Surgery, 4647 Pershing Avenue, St. Louis, Missouri 63108, and ask for a list of accredited plastic surgeons in your region.

What about dermatologists? Do they perform cosmetic operations? How do you find them?

Yes, of the 2,500 qualified dermatologists in the United States, a certain number use minor surgical techniques to deal with some skin problems. Again, extreme care must be used in finding your doctor. Again, the best method is to write or phone your County Medical Society, consult a medical directory of specialists under the heading "Dermatologists," or write to the American Medical Association for their official list.

Once you have a list, what's the next step?

It's always wise to shop around before you decide on a doctor. Your first step should be to phone the practitioners on your list and inquire whether or not they specialize in the type of operation you have in mind. This may eliminate one or two of them right off. Next, you should make appointments with at least two of the others who were not eliminated by the phone call. This may run you $15 to $25 a visit, but it's worth it. You want to have absolute confidence in the person you pick. In this field, trust and understanding between patient and doctor is all-important at every point along the line.

What should you ask the doctor?

Anything and everything you can think of:

cost, risks, procedure, what can and cannot be achieved, how long you will be in the hospital, how long in bandages. Don't hesitate to ask him to show you photographs of the results of similar operations he has performed on other patients. As one cosmetic surgeon puts it: "They should ask everything —they should look before they leap."

What will the doctor ask you?

To start with, he will ask what it is you want done. No, it's not obvious. Picture a flat-chested woman with an enormous nose, protruding ears, and a receding chin, who tells the doctor she has finally made up her mind to have a hidden birthmark removed.

Once the doctor knows your problem, and has examined you, he will want to know your motivation for having the operation. If, for example, a would-be patient brings in a photograph of a movie star and says that she, or he, wants to look like that; or if a woman seems to believe that by having her breasts enlarged or her face lifted, she will save her failing marriage; or if a man appears to be pinning all his hopes for future success on having a more aggressive chin, the doctor may tactfully advise a consultation with a psychiatrist before deciding whether or not to proceed with the operation.

The best motive for having any form of cosmetic surgery done is, in the opinion of most surgeons, simple vanity. If you're changing yourself to please someone else, or because you think that all your troubles will vanish if you look different, you're heading for trouble. It means that you're expecting too much from your operation, and that you may very well be disappointed.

Although many people experience tremendous psychological benefits from correcting a minor abnormality which has troubled them all their lives—or, as with wrinkles, is just beginning to trouble them—others find a change in their appearance oddly difficult to accept. Basically, of course, it's the individual's self-image that is at stake. The doctor must be convinced that patients want the operation solely for their own sake, that they can handle the alteration in their self-image, and that the change will make them feel happier with themselves, more able to enjoy their lives. Indeed, most surgeons agree that the greatest benefit any cosmetic surgery can bestow is to make the patient forget the face or figure problem that has been troubling them. The wisdom of this view is pointed up in a remark made by a girl who'd recently had her nose straightened: "I never think about it anymore. Now I realize how unimportant it was; it's what you are that really matters."

What will the doctor tell you once he's agreed to the operation?

In addition to outlining the procedure, discussing the possible complications, and defining the results he hopes to achieve, he will decide with you when is the best time to do it, set up the dates at the hospital, and arrange to have you photographed. This is usually done by a medical photographer, who will also photograph you after the operation, and costs about $20. The surgeon will also advise you about costs, and request that you pay his fee in advance. This is standard procedure with most cosmetic surgeons.

What about costs? What's the usual range?

The surgeon's fee for most cosmetic operations is somewhere between $500 and $1,500. What you're paying for is not only his technical skill, but also his aesthetic judgment. A good cosmetic surgeon must be something of an artist. His reputation depends on it.

You'll find more details about surgeons' fees for specific operations under their separate headings. Remember that in every case in which hospitalization is required, you must add on hospital fees: room, food, use of operating and recovery rooms, tests, drugs, and anesthetician's fee, among others. Hospital fees vary widely across the country, so it would be impossible to give an average estimate.

Are there any cases in which the fees

can be reduced, or covered by health insurance?

Yes, some surgeons occasionally reduce their fees in serious cases of need, both physical and financial. In addition, there are a number of hospital clinics and teaching colleges at which cosmetic surgery is performed for a fraction of the usual cost. (It's wise to check them out first with the American Board of Plastic Surgery.) In some of these clinics, the operating surgeons are not yet fully qualified plastic surgeons, but are working under the supervision of senior surgeons. In others, like the New York University Hospital, for example, the operating surgeons are fully qualified, and both operation and hospital fees are minimal, especially if the patient is in great need.

Health insurance covers cosmetic surgery only when it is bound up with problems of health or function. Among these operations are nose corrections related to breathing difficulties, and breast alterations related to tissue disorders or back trouble.

The Nose

The term "nose job" is vague. What specific operations does it cover?

Any in which the size or shape of the nose is altered. Cosmetic surgery in this area is used to correct noses that are too large or too long, too short or noticeably crooked, severely humped or depressed at the bridge, excessively hooked or tilted at the tip. Sometimes more than one of these problems is corrected during a single operation.

How are these operations done?

Surprisingly enough, most nose operations are considered major surgery, though they usually require only local anesthetic. In almost every case, they are performed from the inside, through the nostrils, so there is no external scarring whatsoever.

Basically, most nose operations are very

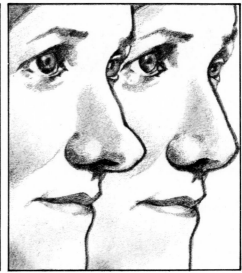

Two types of nose corrections. Right: the smoothing down of a marked arch on the bridge of the nose. Far right: the reduction of the size of the tip.

simple, and take between 45 and 90 minutes. First, the doctor separates the skin from the underlying bone and cartilage. Then, if he is reducing the width, length, or arch of the nose, he uses miniature surgical instruments to cut and reshape the excess bone and cartilage underneath. If he is adding to the length of the nose, or filling in a marked depression on the bridge, he builds it up with a bit of cartilage taken from the rib or behind the ear; a bit of bone from the hip; or a sculpted bit of solid silicone. If he's correcting a bend or twist in the nose, he cuts the bone and resets it straight. The final step in any nose operation is to pack it, splint it, and bandage it.

How long does it take to recover?

The patient is usually in the hospital for about four or five days, and goes home wearing the splint, which comes off at the doctor's office a few days later. For the first 10 to 14 days, the patient's eyes will be black and blue and very bloodshot. A certain amount of facial swelling may remain for up to three months.

Are there any risks involved?

Nose surgery rarely affects the sense of smell adversely, but it can affect breathing for the worse. If it does, a further operation will have to be done to correct the fault. Once it has healed properly, a corrected nose is no more fragile than before the operation.

Will other people notice that you've had your nose altered?

Nine times out of ten, no. Strange to say, people are far less observant than you'd think. They may remark that you look better, but because the change in your looks is a subtle one, they won't know why.

What if you don't like your new nose?

Perfection—even complete satisfaction—is never guaranteed in cosmetic surgery. If you don't like it, you can only have another operation—but of course you'll have to pay, and you can never get your old nose back. For this reason, teenagers are advised to wait a few years before rushing out and having their noses changed. Though a nose attains its major growth by the age of 16 or 17, the face is still changing—gaining in maturity. Sometimes a man or woman realizes only too late that it was their original nose that gave their face distinction.

How much does nose surgery cost?

It depends, of course, on the doctor and on what needs to be done, but usually the surgeon's fee is between $500 and $1,000.

The Chin and Jaw

What kind of chin and/or jaw problems can be corrected by cosmetic surgery?

The most common cosmetic operations in this area are done to correct receding chins, excessively protruding chins and/or jaws, and underchins that are overly fat or flabby. Combination nose and chin operations are becoming more and more frequent, because the relationship between nose and chin is important to facial harmony. Receding chins, or their opposite, overprominent chins, are those most often corrected in tandem with nose surgery.

How is a slightly receding chin corrected?

It's an amazingly simple operation, taking only 15 minutes. With the patient under local anesthetic, the surgeon makes a small slit inside the mouth in front of the teeth, or right under the chin, and inserts a bit of sculpted silicone. If the nose is also being corrected, the surgeon inserts the chin implant first, then alters the nose to harmonize with the new shape of the chin.

What about cases in which the chin or jaw is very underdeveloped or, alternatively, very overdeveloped, as with "lantern jaw"?

Both problems require more lengthy operations—and usually general anesthetic—because the basic bone structure is changed. If the problem is a badly receding chin, the surgeon may have to slide the entire jaw forward, adding to the basic structure of both chin and jaw with bone grafts taken from the patient's hip. If the problem is a prominent chin, in combination with malocclusion (improper bite) or "lantern jaw," the surgeon removes segments of bone from chin and jaw, and slides the jaw back. In both cases, the jaw will have to remain wired in its new position for a period of 6 to 12 weeks. A soft food diet is necessary during this time, and there may be some numbness, which gradually fades.

What about operations to correct doublechins or flabby underchins?

Doublechins are usually corrected as part of a facelift operation. If the problem is simply a pad of fat under the chin, however, or the kind of flabbiness sometimes called "turkey wattle," which may come with age, or after

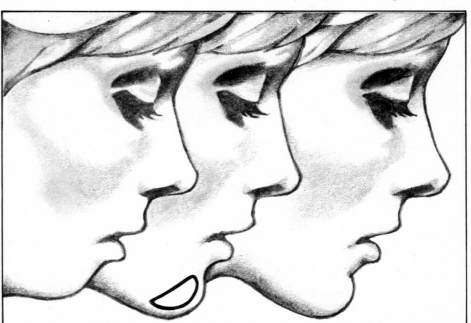

A slightly receding chin can be reshaped with a silicone implant sculpted by the surgeon. The operation is fairly simple.

a rapid weight loss, there is a fairly simple surgical remedy. Performed under local anesthetic, and taking about an hour, it involves the cutting of a Z-shaped incision directly under the chin. Through this incision, the surgeon removes any excess tissue, then cuts away the excess skin and sews it up. The patient can leave the hospital the next day, though he will have to speak through clenched teeth for about a week, and remain on a soft food diet for about two weeks. The scar left by this operation is hardly noticeable.

How much do these chin and/or jaw operations generally cost?

The "Z" operation usually costs between $200 and $500. The silicone implant operation for a slightly receding chin costs between $350 and $750. Correcting a badly receding chin and jaw, or a severely protruding chin and jaw costs between $500 and $1,000. The figure for these more serious operations can be even higher, if the problem is a complex one.

The Ears

Having protruding ears pinned back sounds fairly simple. Exactly how is it done?

Pinning back protruding ears is not really as simple as it sounds. The patient is usually put under general anesthetic, and the operation takes about an hour. After making incisions behind the ears, the surgeon remodels the cartilage in the ears themselves, then stitches them back into place closer to the head. A large, comfortable bandage is placed around the head, and remains on for several days. The stitches are removed after about 10 days, and the patient may be required to wear a light bandage around his head when he goes to bed at night for about three months afterward.

Can ears be reduced in size?

Yes, by surgically removing parts of the cartilage around the outside of the ears and earlobes. This is done in such a way as to create perfectly normal looking, but appreciably smaller ears, and special care is taken to make the incisions in tiny crevices, so that only very small and barely noticeable scars are left. The time spent in the hospital, about two days, and in bandages is about the same as for pinning back the ears. Frequently this "double-trouble" problem—having ears both large and protruding—is corrected in one operation.

What's the best age to have protruding ears corrected?

Any age is all right, but the majority of these operations are performed on children—both boys and girls. For some curious reason, ears reach full growth sooner than almost any other part of the anatomy. A child's ears are fully grown by the time he is eight or nine; the rest of his face slowly "catches up" over the next ten years or so. This can be a real trial for a boy or girl with excessively large or protruding ears. Ultimately, the face may grow sufficiently to harmonize with the size of the ears, but there are many cases, and cosmetic surgeons are the best judges of this, in which the ears will remain disproportionately prominent, no matter how much the face grows. This is especially true, of course, if the child takes after one of his parents with an ear problem. In such cases, doctors usually recommend an operation to pin back the child's ears before he is

"Cup-handle" ears can be corrected before the age of 10, because ears reach full growth very early.

ten, to spare him the taunts and teasing of other children. Unless the child's ears are unusually large, the surgeon will probably suggest waiting a few years before operating to reduce their size, in order to give his face time to catch up with them.

What other ear corrections can be done?

Silicone implants and surgical expertise now make it possible to correct any number of ear problems, from asymmetry (one larger or differently shaped from the other), to ears that flop over at the top, to missing, or malformed ear parts.

Can any of these operations affect hearing?

No, because the outer formation of the ear has nothing to do with hearing. The perception of sounds takes place inside the ear.

How much do ear operations cost?

The surgeon's fee for correcting the outer formation of the ear is usually $350-$600.

Facelifts

What, precisely, is a facelift?

In the simplest terms, it is an operation performed to correct the various facial flaws that appear with age: bags under the eyes; excess skin above the eyes; drooping eyebrows; sagging folds of skin on the cheeks; heavy jowls; and loose, sagging skin on the neck and under the chin. In the full, or standard facelift, all of these signs of aging can be dealt with in a single operation. It is also possible to have a partial facelift— one that corrects sagging in a single area, such as the eyes, cheeks, neck, or jawline. The so-called eyelift is the most popular of these partial facelifts.

Does a facelift erase wrinkles?

Strictly speaking, no. The operation tightens the facial contours, and eliminates sagging folds of skin on various parts of the face, but it cannot iron out wrinkles, or eliminate deep lines, such as those on the forehead, or those that form a sort of parenthesis around the mouth, from nose to chin. A network of fine wrinkles, on the upper lip, for example, can be treated by other means, such as skin planing or peeling. These methods are discussed on pages 138-140.

Is it true that some skin types don't benefit as much from a facelift as others do?

Yes. Thick, heavily pigmented skin does not lend itself well to recontouring. This is also true of very fine, thin skin on a bony face. Skin that has a tendency to heal slowly and leave marked scars is obviously not a good candidate for facial surgery.

What then, are the ideal physical conditions for a facelift operation?

Ideally, the candidate for a facelift should be suffering more from "sags and bags" than from an advanced case of lines and wrinkles. She, or he, should be in good health (facelifts are considered major surgery), and be as close to his or her normal weight as possible. It's not a good idea to have a facelift if you have just lost a lot of weight, or are just about to go on a strict diet.

What's the best age to have a facelift?

Some doctors advise having it done as soon as noticeable sagging begins to appear. Most doctors agree that, in general, the best age is the mid-40's or early 50's, when the skin still retains its tone and elasticity. This is not a hard and fast rule, however; some men and women in their 60's have better skin tone than those in their 30's.

Does a facelift make you look years younger? How long do its benefits last?

The phrase most often used to answer these questions is that a facelift "gives you the jump on a few years." In other words, by smoothing, tightening, and lifting certain areas of the face, it can eliminate the most obvious signs of age, and thus make you look younger. How much younger depends on the individual. No facelift can restore the natural contours of youth, but it can help a person in the early 50's to look 45 or so, or someone in the mid-40's to look 35 or so. Perhaps a facelift is of greatest benefit to those who look older than their years—a woman of 45, for example, who looks 50 or more. In her case, a facelift can help her to look her age, or even a little bit less. The idea is to make the patient look better, and therefore more youthful. It must be remembered, though, that a facelift does not halt the aging process. The benefits achieved are permanent only in that they keep a patient's face looking somewhat younger than that person's actual age. If a person really wants to keep the clock turned back as far as possible, he or she will probably have to have another facelift every 5 to 10 years. This is probably the secret of those movie stars, both male and female, who go on looking 39 or 40 year after year after year.

Will people notice you've had a facelift?

In most cases, no. The change in you will be a subtle one and, unless they're really in the know about such things, they'll simply remark on how much better you look, and probably assume you've had a good vacation. So unless you tell them about it, they'll probably never guess *why* you look better.

How exactly, is a facelift operation performed? What's the procedure?

The operation is usually done under general anesthetic, and takes three to four hours. The surgeon makes a series of incisions inside the hairline at the temple, then down behind the ears and under the earlobes, then back up under the hairline toward the nape of the neck. He then separates the facial skin from the underlying tissue, and gently lifts it up and back, cutting away the surplus skin at the edges, and sometimes making tiny "pleats" in the underlying tissue, before sewing up the incisions. If the patient has a fat or flabby underchin, the surgeon may make a small incision directly under the chin, removing the surplus pad of fat and excess skin before sewing up the incision.

What about lifting the area around the eyes?

Eyelifts can be done as part of the standard facelift, but because this part of the face is

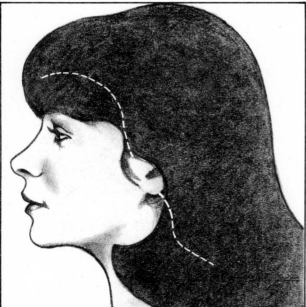

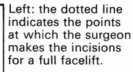
Left: the dotted line indicates the points at which the surgeon makes the incisions for a full facelift.

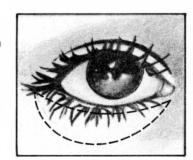

Right: the dotted line shows where the incisions are made for removing bags under the eyes, or folds above it.

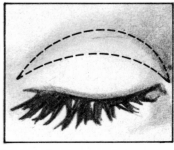

especially delicate, they are often done separately. In fact, a complete eyelift consists of four mini-operations—one each for the upper and lower lid of each eye. The operation is done under local anesthetic, and takes about three hours. The surgeon makes the incisions as close as possible to the eyelashes when removing bags and excess skin from under the eye. The incisions are made in the crease of the lid when the surgeon is removing surplus skin from the area above the eye.

How long do you have to stay in the hospital, and how long in bandages?

The length of time in the hospital can vary from three to seven days. A heavy bandage is worn during this period, and a lighter one for the next 10 days or so, until the stitches are removed at the doctor's office.

Is there much pain? What other risks—such as scarring—are involved?

There's pain, of course, but you neither feel it nor remember it, because immediately after the operation you are given a pain-killing and amnesiac drug called scopolamine. As to the risks involved, they are the same as for any major surgery—only, of course, this is not *necessary* major surgery, so that if any complications do arise, a perfectly healthy person may become an unhealthy one. The risks include hematoma (a swelling containing blood); permanent damage to the skin or facial nerves; thick scars (though in a standard facelift any and all scarring is mostly hidden behind the hairline); infection, or a bad reaction to the drugs administered; temporary numbness of the cheeks or other parts of the face; and temporary, but severe bruising, which may extend as far down as the breasts, or even the waist. With the exception of permanent damage to the skin or facial nerves, which is unlikely at the hands of a skilled and reputable surgeon, all of these complications can be treated at the hospital.

What about using make-up and washing your hair after a facelift?

You can wash and loosely set your hair about a week after a facelift. Light make-up can also be worn at that time. Dark make-up and hair tints should be avoided for at least six weeks; both can irritate and deepen the color of the scars.

How much do facelifts cost?

The standard facelift costs between $750 and $2,000. An eyelift alone costs between $500 and $1,000. A partial facelift, of the temples, cheeks, or jowls, usually costs about $500. Partial facelifts of this type, however, are not advised because their benefits are relatively short, and they can give the face a strange, unharmonious look.

Dermabrasion

What exactly is dermabrasion, and what skin problems is it used to correct?

Dermabrasion works on the same principle as fine sandpaper—it smooths the finish of the skin. A relatively safe and simple operation, it is used both by dermatologists and cosmetic surgeons to reduce scars—whether they be recessed, as in acne scars, or raised, as in the kind of badly-healed scars left over from childhood. Dermabrasion is also used to reduce fine wrinkles, such as those on the upper lip, that are not affected by a facelift. In fact, mild dermabrasion is often used in conjunction with a facelift.

How and where is it done?

It can be done either in the hospital or in the doctor's office. The doctor may use a general or a local anesthetic, or a chemical freeze spray that renders the skin insensitive. To plane down a raised scar, or to even up the differential between a wrinkle or pitted scar and the surrounding area, the doctor uses an electrically operated brush about the size of a dime. Depending on the severity of the problem, the process of planing down the skin may take an hour or just a few minutes.

If the problem is very severe, more than one treatment may be necessary.

How long does it take to recuperate?

The patient goes home the same day wearing a bandage. He is given antibiotics and pills to prevent undue swelling, and is advised to do as little as possible for 24 hours, and to sleep sitting up. The following day, he takes off the bandages, and a scab begins to form on his face. He uses a prescribed ointment to soften it, and, about five days later, begins soaking it with a lukewarm washcloth several times a day. About 10 days after the operation, the scab comes off. The patient's face looks badly sunburned, and feels tender, but both symptoms gradually disappear over the next couple of months. For the first few weeks, the patient is advised not to strain the blood vessels in his face by exerting himself in any way. And for at least six months—even a year—he must protect himself, very, very carefully from sunlight, strong or weak, which can cause a mottled effect on his skin.

Is it true that dermabrasion can be used to stop or lessen acne eruptions?

Yes. Though it would be overoptimistic to say that dermabrasion can cure acne, it does act to inhibit the eruptions. The reason for this is fairly simple. Acne blemishes are infections caused by plugged oil ducts. The longer the ducts, the more readily they become plugged and infected. Dermabrasion, by planing off the outer layer of skin, shortens the ducts and decreases the resistance inside them to the flow of oil. For this reason, dermabrasion is recommended to teenagers suffering from acne, especially if it is severe, and the sooner, the better. Dermabrasion cannot eradicate deeply pitted scars. It is therefore wise to begin dermabrasion treatments before the patient develops the kind of serious facial infections that produce deep scars.

How much does dermabrasion cost?

The usual fee is between $500 and $750. For a partial treatment, the fee may be $150.

Chemopeel

Is this the process that's talked about as the new way to erase wrinkles and scars? If so, how does it differ from dermabrasion?

This is indeed the wrinkle cure offered by some dermatologists and many self-styled "aestheticians." It involves the use of strong chemicals to burn off the outer layer of skin. It differs from dermabrasion in that the brush used to abrade the skin is entirely under the doctor's control, while the chemicals used to burn away the skin are not. The chemopeel process is very painful and extremely dangerous.

Why is it so dangerous?

The chemicals painted on the skin give you a second-degree burn. They can cause severe scarring and permanent change in skin color, with some areas darker, some lighter, than before. They can cause various unpleasant and unsightly eye disorders such as conjunctivitis and inability to close the eyes. Worse still, because they are absorbed through the skin and into the body, they can cause permanent internal damage. Ironically, the more diluted the chemical, the more readily it is absorbed through the skin. Perhaps the most horrifying aspect of these caustic and toxic chemicals is that they may well be carcinogenic—capable of initiating cancer.

Are there any cases in which the chemopeel process is relatively safe?

Possibly only when the chemical is used in minute quantities, by a reputable cosmetic surgeon, to reduce wrinkles in a confined area, such as the upper lip, in connection with a surgical facelift. Most doctors, however, are extremely wary of this process. As one well-known cosmetic surgeon puts it: "There isn't anything chemosurgery can do that dermabrasion can't do as well—or better."

How is a full-face chemopeel done?

The chemical (usually phenol, a form of carbolic acid) is painted on the face, section by section. As the skin is treated, it turns frosty white, then deep red. A mask of tape is applied to the face, and for the next 48 hours, the patient is asked not to speak or move her face. She sips a liquid diet through a straw. After 48 hours, the tape is removed, and a hard brown crust begins to form. The patient dusts her face every few hours with a white antiseptic powder, and uses petroleum jelly to soften the crust, which peels off after about a week. Though the treatment can be done in a doctor's office, a stay of about five to seven days in the hospital is advisable, considering the possibility of complications. When the crust comes off, the face will be bright pink, tender, and swollen—symptoms which should fade away over the next few weeks. Provided there are no complications, the patient's face will look smoother as a result of the peel.

How much pain is there?

The patient is given sedatives and pain-killers, but no anesthetic. The pain, from the moment the acid is applied, to the moment the tape is taken off, and even after that, is excruciating. "My skin felt on fire," says one woman. "It was constant pain," says another. "If my doctor hadn't been so reassuring," says a third, "I'd have been frightened to death by the pain."

How much does chemopeel cost?

A full-face chemopeel can cost $500-$1,000 if done by a doctor or dermatologist. Non-medical "aestheticians" can—and often do—charge as much as $3,000 for this treatment.

Breast Enlargement

What's the typical candidate for breast enlargment usually like?

Despite the publicity they receive, the topless waitress and apsiring actress types make up only a small percentage of the women seeking this type of surgery. By far the majority are average women between the ages of 18 and 38, married or unmarried, working or bringing up children. They go to a cosmetic surgeon not because they want to have the dimensions of Raquel Welch (they're advised to see a psychiatrist if they do), but because their breasts are excessively small, and they want to look more "normal." In some cases, their breasts are not merely very small, but practically non-existent. Indeed, a few of them are as flat-chested as a boy, with the sole exception that their nipples are female, and, of course, connected to milk-producing glands. There are also some cases in which one of the breasts has failed to develop—an acute case of the asymmetry common to us all. In most cases, it's only the woman herself who worries about her breasts; her husband or boyfriend loves her just as she is. In fact, these are the cases most acceptable to the cosmetic surgeon. He will be extremely reluctant to operate on a woman if larger breasts are her husband's or boyfriend's idea of acceptability. Even given a loving husband or boyfriend, women with very underdeveloped breasts suffer from our cultural prejudices. Since the turn of the century, such women have been willing to undergo all manners of daring—and often disastrous—medical experiments in an effort to acquire bigger proportions.

What sort of techniques have been tried?

The first was to transplant sections of the patient's own tissue from the buttocks to the breasts. This didn't work too well for two reasons: first, women with small breasts tended to be slender all over, so there wasn't much surplus tissue to transplant; second, in its new location, the transplanted tissue tended to be reabsorbed by the body. The next method tried was to inject liquid paraffin into the breasts. This was soon abandoned when it became clear that the paraffin tended to form nodules in the breast and encouraged the formation of tumors. In the

1950's, plastic "open pore" sponges were introduced, and surgeons began using them as breast implants. Again, no success: sooner or later, these sponges became impacted with fibrous tissue, shrank drastically, and grew hard as a rock. Then in the early 1960's, came liquid silicone. Thousands of women had their breasts made larger by this method before the dire consequences began to appear. Liquid silicone has an unfortunate tendency to travel, especially when injected in large quantities. It could end up anywhere in the body—such as in the groin, or even the knees. There were a few horrifying cases in which it entered the bloodstream and caused blindness, heart and lung failure. Worse, if possible, the presence of liquid silicone in the tissue made cancer detection impossible. In 1965, the Food and Drug Administration stepped in and made the use of liquid silicone illegal.

What about the gel-filled sac implant?

This is the newest and most sophisticated method of breast enlargement. Invented in 1965 by a surgeon named Tom Cronin, it consists of a cone-shaped plastic bag filled with silicone gel and backed with dacron mesh. It comes in eight sizes, and its insertion is fairly simple. The operation takes about two hours and is done under general anesthetic. The surgeon makes a three-inch incision below the curve of the breast, or below the point where a fully developed breast would curve. He then separates the existing breast tissue from the chest wall, and slips the implant into the pocket thus formed, with the dacron mesh flush against the chest wall. After sewing up this incision, he makes another, in the breast tissue itself, and inserts a small tube which will be used to drain off excess fluid after the operation. This is one advantage of the Cronin method over its predecessors—the accumulation of fluid inside the breast was a major problem with the sponge technique. Other advantages of the Cronin method include the dacron mesh backing, which anchors the implant to the chest wall as the patient's own tissue

fibers grow into it; the self-adherent quality of the gel, which ensures that, even if the bag gets torn in an accident, the silicone will not travel; and the positioning of the implant behind the patient's own tissue, which makes cancer detection possible.

How long does it take to recuperate?

The patient is in the hospital for about five days. For the first 48 hours, she is heavily bandaged and required not to move her arms. Then, any excess fluid is drained off, the tubes sealed, folded back under the implant, and the small incisions closed. A light dressing is applied, which the patient wears, along with a supportive bra, day and night for the next three weeks, when the stitches are taken out. During this time, the patient is cautioned against raising her arms, except for such actions as eating or gently combing her hair. After that, she can begin using them for driving, and other light movements, but is asked to avoid strenuous activity for two months.

What are the risks of scarring, cancer, or other ill effects?

The scars are fairly well hidden under the curve of the breast. The risk of cancer seems to be no greater after the implant than before. But there may be complications, for this is, after all, a major operation. Among these are blood clotting, excessive fluid accumulation, and infection—with accompanying pain, fever, and swelling. All these complications can be dealt with in the hospital. Excessive firmness, sagging, or assymmetry will have to be corrected with further surgery.

Will the implant look and feel natural? Can a woman nurse a baby afterward?

Provided there are no complications, the answer to these questions is yes, because the implant is behind the woman's own tissue. The sensory nerves and milk-producing glands go on functioning as before.

How much does this operation cost?

The usual fee is between $750 and $1,500.

Breast Reduction

Isn't this an operation that can be done for reasons of health as well as appearance?

Decidedly yes. Women with excessively large and pendulous breasts—each weighing as much as four pounds or more—are carrying a heavy burden in an awkward position. Prevented by the size of their bosom from engaging in any strenuous activities, they are nonetheless more than usually prone to fatigue and serious back ailments. They sometimes have trouble sleeping, and often suffer from skin irritations, both below the breasts and on the shoulders, where the bra straps cut into the flesh. All this is in addition to the embarrassment of "having too much of a good thing," and the difficulty of finding clothes that fit. Cosmetic surgeons are generally sympathetic to this problem, and rarely question the advisability of performing a corrective operation.

What's the best age to have it done?

The operation can be performed at any age after 16 or 17. Some 80 per cent of the women who have this problem have had it since puberty, and the operation is often performed on girls still in their teens. Breast reduction is even more commonly sought by women in their 20's, 30's, 40's, and 50's—women who have only just discovered that something can be done to help them.

How is the operation done?

Though in principle it is a fairly simple operation, the techniques employed are more complex than for breast enlargement. It is done under general anesthetic, and takes four to five hours. The surgeon makes an incision like an upside-down "T" under the curve of the breast and up to the nipple. Through this incision, he excises the surplus tissue and then cuts away the excess skin. In many cases, it is also necessary to reposition the nipple. This is done by cutting a round of skin the same size as the nipple area, but higher up on the breast, and grafting the nipple into its new position.

How long does it take to recuperate?

The patient is usually in the hospital for about 10 days, and remains heavily bandaged for about three weeks, when the stitches are taken out. During this time, she is advised not to use her arms more than is strictly necessary, and must wear a supportive brassiere, day and night, for about three months.

What complications can there be?

Cancer, which worries women most, seems to be no more likely after this operation than before it. As with the breast implant operation, there may be infection, and some pain. Perhaps the most serious complication that can arise is the loss of a nipple through infection. Other, less serious complications are loss of feeling in the nipples, or loss of feeling in other parts of the breasts. In most cases, sensation returns six months or so after the operation.

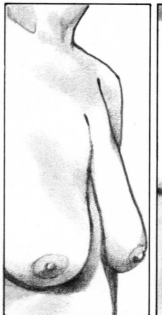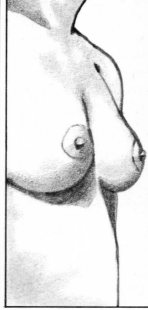

Modern surgical techniques now make it possible to achieve a dramatic reduction in breast size.

Is there a noticeable scar?

Yes. This is unavoidable, because the incision is not confined to the area just under the breasts, but goes right up to the nipple. The incision around the repositioned nipple itself is far less noticeable. In any case, many women seem to prefer a scar on the surface to the problem of oversize.

How much does breast reduction cost?

The usual fee is between $750 and $1,500.

Body Lifts

What exactly does a body lift mean?

This is a catchall phrase covering several techniques currently being used to reduce fat and flab from various parts of the body: the upper arms and thighs, the buttocks and the stomach. Some relatively thin people resort to a body lift when they find they can't lose excess fat or flab from a particular area through diet and exercise.

What about heavy, flabby upper arms?

The correction of this so-called bat-wing problem usually requires two separate operations, one for each arm, about a month apart. The operations can take about two hours each, and consist in the cutting out of a section of tissue and skin on the inner side of the arm. If it's simply hanging skin that is being removed, the patient may not need a dressing, but only a plastic spray, to keep the incision closed. If tissue is being removed as well, a dressing will be required until the stitches are removed, about two weeks after the operation.

What about reducing the size of the thighs?

This is a more complex operation than the arm lift, and can take four to five hours. The surgeon makes an incision down the inside of the thigh, through which he excises the surplus tissue. Then he cuts away any excess skin, and sews up the incision. The patient is in the hospital for about a week, and must keep the legs elevated for the first three days. He wears bandages on his legs for about two or three weeks—until the stitches are removed.

Can you have your bottom lifted along with the thigh lift?

Yes. But the two operations will be done separately, and the whole thing will require a stay of about two weeks in the hospital. The buttock lift takes about two hours, and, as with the arm and leg lifts, is done under general anesthetic. The incisions are made in the fold of the seat. Through these incisions, the surgeon removes surplus fat and then cuts away the excess skin. Again, bandages are worn for about two weeks.

What about reducing the size of the stomach?

This operation is also done under general anesthetic, and the patient is kept in the hospital for about a week. A vertical or horizontal incision is made in the abdomen, the surplus tissue removed, and the excess skin cut away before the incision is sewn up. The patient goes home wearing bandages. Even after the stitches are taken out, a support bandage may have to be worn for several months after the operation.

What about the possibility of complications?

As most of these operations are considered major surgery, the possible complications are the same as for any major surgery: infection, swelling, and blood clotting. For this type of cosmetic surgery, however, complications are rare. The main difficulty is scarring, wherever the incisions are made—inside the arms or thighs, under the buttocks, or on the abdomen. There is no way to avoid scars.

How much do body lifts cost?

The usual fee for a thigh or buttock lift is between $750 and $2,000. For an arm lift, it is usually $500-$1,000. Stomach reduction usually costs about $1,000.

143

For Your Bookshelf

Eileen Ford's Book of Model Beauty
Trident Press (New York: 1968; Seventh Printing, 1971)

Beauty is no big deal
by Donna Lawson and Jean Conlon, Bernard Geis Associates (New York: 1971)

Your Skin and Hair: A Basic Guide to Care and Beauty
by Earle W. Brauer, M.D., The Macmillan Company (New York: 1969; Third Printing, 1971)

Organic Make-up: The Natural Way to Beauty
by Mary Gjerde, Nash Publishing Corporation (Los Angeles: 1971)

The Complete Book of Hair Styles, Beauty and Fashion
by Miriam Cordwell and Marion Rudoy, Crown Publishers, Inc. (New York: 1971)

Stay Young Longer
by Linda Clark, M.A., Pyramid Books, Inc. (New York: 1961; Tenth Printing, 1971)

Aerobics
by Kenneth Cooper, M.D., M.P.H., Major, U.S.A.F. Medical Corps, Bantam Books, Inc. (New York: 1968)

Yoga for Beauty and Health
by Eugene Rawls and Eve Diskin, Parker Publishing Company, Inc. (West Nyack, N.Y.: 1968; Third Printing, 1970)

Cosmetic Surgery
by William E. Brown, Stein and Day Publishers (New York)

The Skin Game: Beauty Secrets the "Experts" Don't Want You to Know
by Colette Dowling, J.B. Lippincott Company (Philadelphia and New York: 1971)

Plastic Surgery: Beauty You Can Buy
by Harriet La Barre, Dell Publishing Company, Inc. (New York: 1972)

Picture Credits